Teams

Learning to work effectively and efficiently in a group is an important part of learning to be a substantive contributor in today's environment. *Teams: A Competency-Based Approach* provides solid coverage of the underlying theory, complemented by examples, to help students learn how systematically to identify, analyze, and manage issues that arise as a result of teamwork. With exercises and activities designed to allow students to engage with the material and build specific team-oriented competencies, this book offers readers the tools needed for successful group experiences.

Consuelo M. Ramirez, Ph.D. is a Senior Lecturer with the Department of Management in the College of Business of the University of Texas at San Antonio, USA.

Teams
A Competency-Based Approach

Consuelo M. Ramirez, PhD

Routledge
Taylor & Francis Group

NEW YORK AND LONDON

First published 2014
by Routledge
711 Third Avenue, New York, NY 10017

and by Routledge
2 Park Square, Milton Park, Abingdon, Oxon OX14 4RN

Routledge is an imprint of the Taylor & Francis Group, an informa business

Library of Congress Cataloging-in-Publication Data
Ramirez, Consuelo.
Teams : a competency based approach / Consuelo Ramirez, Ph.D.
    pages cm
  Includes bibliographical references and index.
  1. Teams in the workplace.   I. Title.
  HD66.R35   2013
  658.4'022—dc23   2013015307

ISBN: 978-0-415-89986-4 (hbk)
ISBN: 978-0-415-89987-1 (pbk)
ISBN: 978-0-203-15604-9 (ebk)

Typeset in Adobe Garamond Pro
by Apex CoVantage, LLC

Printed and bound in the United States of America by
Edwards Brothers Malloy

I dedicate my book to Pearl with heartfelt gratitude for the unconditional love, trust, respect, encouragement and support. A simple thank you is simply not enough.

About the Author

Consuelo M. Ramirez, PhD, is a senior lecturer with the Department of Management in the College of Business of the University of Texas at San Antonio. Dr. Ramirez began her teaching career at UTSA in the Fall of 2000, where she also served as assistant dean for undergraduate studies. In addition to her administrative and teaching duties, she served as advisor to the Students in Free Enterprise organization and the Business Scholars Program. She is known for her mentoring and support of undergraduate students.

Prior to her employment at UTSA, she worked in the corporate environment for 25 years for Fortune 500 and Top 100 Fortune Companies. Her positions in the corporate workforce included duties as a manager, consultant, personal coach, project manager and facilitator in leadership and organization development. Additional work experience includes positions in the public school system and nonprofit organizations. She holds a bachelor's degree in education from Texas Woman's University, a master's in education from Texas Tech University and a doctorate in leadership studies from Our Lady of the Lake University. Dr. Ramirez has also earned a Senior Professional in Human Resources designation and multiple Who's Who Among Teachers in American Colleges and Universities awards.

Dr. Ramirez uses her extensive work experience and academic background to draw from in her publications. Her research interests include team building, ethics and social responsibility, organization behavior and humor in the workforce.

Contents

Introduction

Nobody works alone.

This book is based on years of practical experience in the corporate work environment as well as years of academic experience. Corporate America tends to hire entry-level employees with a minimum requirement of a bachelor's degree and two to three years of work experience. Typically, a bachelor's degree is the culmination of four years of theory, lectures and academic research papers. The work experience for most entry-level employees usually includes temporary positions and other menial jobs that help students support themselves while attending universities. Schools and businesses focus on the cognitive skills that a person needs for successful completion of work. When employees enter the workforce, their greatest challenge is to blend the theories they have learned in school and the limited work experience they have in order to meet the needs and expectations of the organization. This is why it is so important to learn a practical approach to meeting those needs. This practical approach, centered on the soft skills needed in the workplace, is what this book is about.

Most individuals who have worked in organizations or attended school or belonged to religious groups or . . . the list can go on forever . . . have probably been a member of a team or work group of some type. Some group experiences are fruitful and some group experiences are not. Nevertheless, all group experiences present unique challenges. This book is designed to help individuals identify, learn and practice competencies that will help improve their group experiences and turn them into team-building opportunities. Both immediate and long-term benefits of building effective teams are directly related to improved productivity for the individual, the team and the organization. The benefits of effective teams apply equally to small teams, large teams, entrepreneurs, or companies of any size.

Many group experiences fail because members of the group are unable to identify, analyze and manage issues that are inherent to working with others toward a common goal. If a group of individuals were to identify, analyze and manage issues while working with others toward a common goal, they would be a team. This we know, that groups are not teams.

Effective teamwork requires the synergy of knowledge, skills and abilities. Collectively knowledge, skills and abilities can develop into well-defined competencies. A competency is a simultaneous existence of the knowledge, skills and abilities required for effectiveness in individual, group, team and/or organizational performance.[1] A competency-based approach is critical to the development of effective teams. This book will provide theory and application exercises to help individuals learn how to systematically identify, analyze and manage issues that arise as a result of teamwork. It can be difficult to work in a group, but learning to work effectively and efficiently in a group is an important part of learning to be a substantive contributor in today's environment by asking questions, such as What or why is it that certain things happen? Why is it important? What can I do about it? What have I learned from the experience?

People are the common denominator in every group or team. An individual's competencies are an important requirement for effectiveness in a group or team. The competencies needed in group or teamwork shift the requirements of knowledge, skills and abilities to a different standard.[2] In addition to the difference between working alone and working in a group or team, today's organizations are increasingly team based and complex in the demands they place on performance and productivity.[3]

How to Use This Book

The contents of this book have application value to anyone involved in higher education, corporate training, continuing education, consulting or independently pursuing knowledge. Although there are no prerequisites for using this book, it is important to realize that the contents include a wide variety of exercises and activities that do rely on some expectation of knowledge in the topic of teambuilding. Regardless of the level of knowledge, skill or ability in working with others, the expected outcome of using this book is to enhance the soft skills needed in working effectively in teams.

The 10 Essential Competencies for Excelling in a Team-Based Environment:

1 Building relationships: The human side of teamwork.
2 Inner-self competency: What you bring to a team environment.
3 Diversity competency: What you need to know about today's workforce.
4 Team competency: What you need to know about the team environment.

5   Communication competency: Social networks and communicating effectively in the team environment.

6   Environment competency: Matching the needs of the organization.

7   Business ethics & social responsibility competency: Sustainability in today's workplace.

8   Decision-making competency: Critical thinking for consistently making each decision the best decision.

9   Time-Management Competency: The tool kit for effectiveness and efficiency.

10   Lifelong Learning Competency: The key to future success.

You will see the following model illustrated throughout this book. The model serves to illustrate the importance of the 10 essential competencies for excelling in a team-based environment. Although the essential competencies are presented in a sequential manner for learning purposes, once acquired, the competencies are free flowing and intermingling, depending on the needs of each unique situation.

The 10 Essential Competencies for Excelling in a Team-Based Environment:

Figure 0.1

Themes that provide context for the 10 Essential Competencies: The subject matter in this book weaves through four areas of concern: The Individual, The Group, The Environment, and Tools for Success. These themes provide context for the materials as an anchor for the content.

Theme 1: The Individual

Objective: To help the individual recognize opportunities in which she/he will work with others to accomplish goals. This objective will help individuals:

- Identify personal notions about working in groups.
- Compare and contrast individual differences.
- Assess own strengths and weaknesses regarding group work.
- Apply lessons in individual exercises.
- Apply lessons in small-group activities.
- Apply lessons in large-group (classroom) activities.
- Reflect on future applications in written assignments.
- Apply lessons to future group discussions.
- Conduct a wrap-up of lessons learned.

Theme 2: The Group

Objective: To help the individual appreciate other individual's attributes in group settings. This objective will help individuals:

- Identify generational differences.
- Understand group dynamics.
- Conduct research on group dynamics.
- Assess own strengths and weaknesses regarding group dynamics. Emphasis is on honoring our weaknesses as development opportunities.
- Apply lessons in individual exercises.
- Apply lessons in small-group activities.
- Apply lessons in large-group (classroom) activities.
- Reflect on future applications in written assignments.

Theme 3: The Environment

Objective: To help the individual analyze and apply the types of environments in which group/team work is most advantageous. This objective will help individuals:

- Conduct research on successful and unsuccessful group/team environments.
- Compare and contrast research findings in individual exercises.

- Compare and contrast research findings in small-group activities.
- Compare and contrast research findings in large-group (classroom) activities.
- Reflect on future applications in written assignments.

Theme 4: Tools for Success

Objective: To help the individual recognize and build competencies in areas that leverage successful group experiences. This objective will help individuals:

- Ask if they are a good match for group work.
- Recognize the differences between individuals and honor them.
- Know the best practices in technology that are useful for group communication.
- Improve time-management skills.
- Recognize and manage conflict.
- Practice appropriate personal and business ethics.
- Build relationships effectively.
- Practice appropriate humor skills.

Every organization creates complex problems as a result of the interactions between people, processes and structures.[4] A 2006 survey of 461 business leaders reported the most necessary, and yet lacking, business skills for today's workforce that help organizations gain a competitive advantage; they include professionalism (work ethic), communications skills, collaboration (teamwork) skills and problem-solving skills (critical thinking).[5] This book's contents are designed to create opportunities to improve conceptual, communication and other interpersonal skills through the application of team building and conflict management theories and best practices.

Effective business environments require timely application of knowledge and clear thinking, effective communication, and the ability to work with others as a member of a group or team. These requirements are supported here by including experiential learning exercises as a mechanism to develop conceptual and thinking skills. These exercises are designed to engage the individual in activities that will help them learn how to find and use resources for multiple applications. Simply stated, experiential learning is based on learning from our experiences through an iterative process that includes reasoning, evaluation, reflection and practice.[6]

The Process

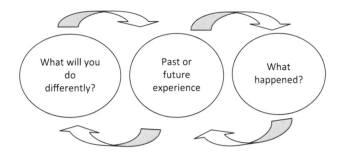

Figure 0.2

The Result: Learning

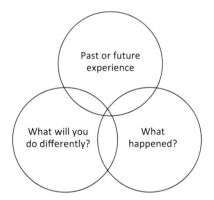

Figure 0.3

The ultimate expected outcome is that the individual will acquire a curiosity about learning by asking questions and seeking answers. It is important that individuals in the business environment learn about themselves and their capacity for working effectively with others. These are perhaps the most important outcomes that will result from reading and using the contents of this book. Adult learning theory further supports this approach to learning about working with others by stating that adults learn best when:

- They are involved in the learning.
- They can use their experiences, good ones and bad ones.

- They can find immediate applications to their lives.
- They can use the information to solve problems as opposed to just memorizing the educational materials.[7]

The learning principles listed above are part of the foundation for experiential learning, and these work better with adult learners than the more traditional approaches, such as lectures and other content-centered learning experiences.

Notes

1. Hellriegel, D., & Slocum, J. W. (2011). *Organizational behavior.* Mason, OH: South-Western Cengage Learning.
2. Morgeson, F. P., Reider, M. H. & Campion, M. A. (2005). Selecting individuals in team settings: The importance of social skills, personality characteristic, and teamwork knowledge. *Personnel Psychology, 58,* 583–611.
3. Rapp, T., Maynard, M. T., Mathieu, J. & Gilson, L. (2008). Team effectiveness 1997–2007: A review of recent advancements and a glimpse into the future. *Journal of Management, 34*(3), 410–476.
4. Smith, M. K. (2001). David A. Kolb on experiential learning. *The encyclopedia of informal education.* Retrieved from http://infed.org/mobi/david-a-kolb-on-experiential-learning/
5. *Are they really ready to work? Employers' perspectives on the basic knowledge and applied skills of new entrants to the 21st century U.S. workforce.* (2006). The Conference Board, Corporate Voices for Working Families, the Partnership for 21st Century Skills, and the Society for Human Resource Management. Retrieved from http://www.p21.org/storage/documents/FINAL_REPORT_PDF09-29-06.pdf
6. Hellriegel & Slocum.
7. Conlan, J., Grabowski, S., & Smith, K. (2003). Adult learning. In M. Orey (Ed.), *Emerging perspectives on learning, teaching, and technology.*

Building Relationships

The Human Side of Teamwork

I've learned that you shouldn't go through life with a catcher's mitt on both hands; you need to be able to throw something back.

—Maya Angelou*

Introduction

Chapter 1 introduces the cornerstone of teams—the relationships between two or more individuals. Training and education programs tend to focus on the cognitive skills needed to complete tasks and achieve goals. Working with others toward a common goal requires an additional skill that is based on developing interpersonal and intrapersonal relationships. This chapter contains exercises and activities designed to help the reader reflect on and

---

Chapter 1 Competencies

The purpose of this chapter is to help you:

- Identify and describe the human side of teamwork.
- Know and understand the role of interpersonal skills.
- Analyze the correlation between teamwork and other social relationships.

Figure 1.1

assess his or her own views first. After the self-reflection, additional exercises and activities incorporate others into the process of developing the needed skills for building relationships in the work environment.

The Difference Between Groups and Teams

Groups and teams are comprised of a consistent component: people. The difference between a team and a group lies primarily in the way the individual members share a common goal. In a team, member's contributions synergize to produce a collective deliverable; while in a group, member's individual contributions might be stronger.[1] Many team-building models describe the importance of the skills that are necessary for the completion of a given task or objective. Team-building models illustrate the components of a team based on strategic goals, departmental goals and work-unit goals.[2] After all, the success of the organization is based on accomplishing the goals set by upper management. These organizational models tend to support strong competency sets to generate product or service deliverables. It is a customary practice to dedicate subject-matter experts and other skilled resources to such goal-directed teams; yet, they are weak in interpersonal skills.

While group members are skilled in the delivery of products and/or services, the missing link is often the development of relationships between the members of the group or team. Relationships are built through learning, developing and practicing interpersonal skills. Unfortunately, business-school curriculums tend to emphasize quantitative and qualitative skills much more than they do interpersonal skills.[3] Failure to learn and develop interpersonal skills is a missed opportunity. The following scenario and exercises provide an introduction to the type of self-development activities that can lead to effective and efficient group work. The fundamental concept lies in our ability to learn. When people learn, they make changes in what they know and how they behave. Practice and experience are the primary drivers of learning.[4]

Exercise: Identifying Interpersonal Skills

Imagine most departmental meetings—a business social event or a project and the coworkers involved in each event. Remember the people who were present, the conversations and the dynamics in general. While some of the memories might be pleasant, there are undoubtedly other memories that were less memorable. Complete the following exercise in the context of your recent encounters with others, as stated previously. Divide your examples between best and worst group experiences.

List the best group experiences (e.g., meeting, social event, project):

1

2

3

List the worst group experiences (e.g., meeting, social event, project):

1

2

3

The best and worst experiences listed previously are most likely described by the event itself, such as your organization's anniversary, achievements, new programs or a holiday business event. Now, take a moment to identify the reason for each reaction. In the next exercise, briefly describe why the event was memorable for each category. What happened that made the event a positive or negative event?

Describe the *best* group experiences listed in the previous exercise. Answer the question: What made the experience successful (e.g., I met new coworkers.)?

1

2

3

Describe the *worst* group experiences listed in the previous exercise. Answer the question: What made the experience less than successful (e.g., lack of organization)?

1

2

3

Reflect on your *best* and *worst* group experiences by comparing the two, and write a statement about how each best experience might influence a similar future event.

Table 1.1

My *best* group experiences have influenced the desired outcome of a future event by (e.g., I plan to stay in touch with my coworkers.):
1
2
3

Now, review your *worst* group experiences. How could you improve each situation? Write a statement for each worst experience to describe your improvements.

Table 1.2

My *worst* group experiences will help to improve future events by (e.g., I will contribute ideas for schedules and events.):
1
2
3

This exercise tends to generate descriptions of interpersonal skills-based issues over knowledge, skills or abilities that are specific to the event. The relationship issues include a wide range of concerns. The following is a list of examples of common interpersonal issue concerns. Mark all of the items that apply to your individual situation. Then compare your results with a colleague or coworker to determine common areas of concern.

- Lack of contact information.
- Lack of ground rules and other agreements.
- Lack of understanding of an individual's priorities regarding social circumstances, such as family, commitments, and so on.
- Time-management concerns.
- Logistical concerns regarding when and where to meet.
- Failure to discuss conflict-management views.
- Failure to discuss consequences of behavior.

Summary Questions:

1   What did you learn from the exercise?

2   How many common concerns did you and a partner identify?

3   Which common concerns were you able to resolve? How?

4   If you were not able to resolve some concerns, why not?

5   Will this exercise help you in future group or team interactions? How?

Interpersonal Skills in the Work Environment

Why is working in groups/teams, at the very least, challenging? Tim Bryce, a corporate consultant of 30 years offers his opinion of the fundamental reason for the challenges of working in groups: "In the United States there is more of a natural inclination to teach individualism as opposed to teamwork; perhaps this is because we are a nation based on freedoms."[5] It is no surprise that issues exist; the focus needs to be on solutions. It is hard to believe that anyone approaches each workday with the intention of making mistakes, hating the work environment or the people with whom he/she works. Yet, this happens every day in the workplace. The reality lies in the failure to acknowledge and address behavioral issues in the workplace. Studies support the theory that the return on investment of group and team work is not realized when there is a lack of balance between technical, professional and interpersonal skills.[6] After all, we are not computers, and, even then, computers are not infallible.

A simple yet powerful and fundamental approach to building relationships in all aspects of life is to separate each interpersonal experience into two distinct and parallel dimensions. Every interpersonal transaction has two distinct dimensions or components: a human component and a business component. The degree of success in achieving the business component of an interaction is directly related to how the human portion of the exchange is approached. Studies suggest that the success of achieving a business goal improves when an individual approaches the event on the human side or with well-developed interpersonal skills.[7]

The illustration that follows is a conceptual interpretation of a typical example of a scenario as described in the previous paragraphs:

Interpersonal/Business Transaction Model

Figure 1.2

Exercise: Interpersonal/Business Transaction

Assume you are assigned to work with a new group/team, and you meet a group/team member during your initial meeting. Using the interpersonal/business transaction model, how would you begin your working relationship?

Example

There is no right or wrong way to complete this exercise. The intention of the exercise is to raise your awareness about how you usually approach a business interaction and to suggest that initiation of this interaction on the human side might improve your success in achieving your desired business goal. An example for this exercise could be that you want to exchange contact information. The exchange for this example follows.

Goal of the Interaction: Exchange Contact Information

| Begin with the human component by saying: Hello, I've been assigned to this group/team. My name is Ann. What is your name? | Merge into the business component by saying: Let's exchange contact information so we can stay in touch between meetings. | Exit the transaction with the human component by saying: I'm happy to meet you, and I look forward to working together. |

Figure 1.3

Now, practice and describe your proposed interaction with your group/team member by writing comments in the spaces below.

Goal of Interaction: _____

Once you establish this pattern, practice so the interchange becomes less scripted and more natural. Other examples of ice-breaking types of exchanges in a group/team setting will follow in another exercise.

Developing interpersonal skills does not have to be a painstaking undertaking. Some potential group/team members might view the development of interpersonal skills as too "touchy-feely" and a waste of time. These types of interpersonal exercises might even remind some participants of group therapy that requires emotional openness. Some individuals prefer to spend valuable time addressing the task or deliverable that needs to be produced. The purpose of highlighting the value of learning interpersonal skills is to raise awareness in view of the validated success reported in research, studies and surveys

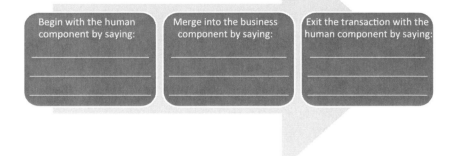

| Begin with the human component by saying: | Merge into the business component by saying: | Exit the transaction with the human component by saying: |

Figure 1.4

of numerous corporate employees. Employees are not therapists nor are they psychologists, and that type of work should be left to the experts. Interpersonal skills are, nevertheless, another tool that can be used to leverage business success. Abraham Maslow's research supports this notion: "If all you have is a hammer, then everything looks like a nail."[8]

Exercise: Interpersonal-Skills Awareness

Where should an individual start to develop interpersonal skills that will serve as tools for successful business interactions? One suggestion is to start by developing self-awareness to determine a baseline on which to build competencies.

What is your baseline? Use the following questions as a self-assessment tool to determine your own baseline with regard to interpersonal-skill awareness. Once you answer the following questions, you can also use the example questions in a group or team setting as practice and for future development opportunities.

Answer each question from your own perspective in the context of working with others in a group setting. The context might include a business, social, family or academic environment.

Self-Assessment: Interpersonal-Skills Awareness

Answer each question candidly based on your group or teamwork experiences:

1   Do you prefer detailed or general types of assignments?
2   Is your schedule flexible or set?

3   Do you prefer meeting before, during or after lunch?

4   Describe your experience in working with groups/teams?

5   Do you prefer to work alone or with others?

6   What strengths do you bring to the group/team?

7   What do you do well?

8   What skills do you want to develop?

9   Is there anything on which you would rather not work?

10   How much time should you spend in a meeting?

11   Do you prefer to talk or to listen?

This list of sample questions can include many and any topics related to individual preferences that are essential to group work. Once you assess your own preferences and practices, you can then take the first opportunity with a group or team member to discuss these types of personal characteristics. Then you begin to establish a common setting for what is to follow. You have established a path toward learning about and with your group/teammates. Other relevant questions for follow-up might include, but are not limited to, the following:

1   What do you want to accomplish individually as you work on this assignment?

2   What do you want to accomplish as a group while you work on this assignment?

3   What might get in the way of achieving your personal goals?

4   What might get in the way of achieving group/team goals?

5   What type of meeting schedule can we set?

6   Where should we meet?

7   What are attendance expectations and/or requirements?

8   Who prepares the agenda for meetings?

9   When will assignments be due?

10   What are the consequences for unmet assignment due dates?

11   How will you communicate and how often?

12   What potential conflicts might arise among or between group/team members?

13   How will the group members deal with conflict?

14   How will we provide each other with ongoing feedback? How often?

15   Should the group/team members complete evaluations on each other; when?

Add any other questions relevant to this topic in the following spaces:

16

17

18

19

20

Knowing yourself is the foundation for continuous improvement and learning on numerous levels: individual work, group work, and teamwork. Self-reflection is where it all begins to take shape in that it allows an individual to learn from past successes and failures.[9]

The first chapter's objective intends to put the individual's past experiences into perspective when it comes to working with others toward a common goal; the big picture.

Chapter 2, The Inner-Self Competency, covers what you bring to a team environment. The content and exercises will continue to focus on the individual. Yet, the purpose is to begin with steps that might lead to a positive and productive greater good without losing the benefits at the individual level.

Review Questions

1   Compare and contrast the human side of teamwork and the business side of teamwork.

2   Define interpersonal skills and why these are important skills in group and team environments.

3   Analyze the correlation between teamwork and other social relationships.

Note: Answers to the review questions are located in the Appendix.

Notes

* Thursby, Jacqueline S. (2011). *Critical companion to Maya Angelou*. New York: Infobase Publishing. Ebook Library. Web. 01 May. 2013.

1. Daft, R. L. (1999). *Leadership theory and practice*. Orlando, FL: Harcourt Brace & Company.

2. Thompson, L. L. (2004). *Making the team*. Upper Saddle River, NJ: Pearson.

3. Robbins, S. P., & Hunsaker, P. L. (2012). *Training in interpersonal skills*. Boston, MA: Prentice Hall.
4. Hellriegel, S. & Slocum, J. W. (2009). *Organizational Behavior* (13th Ed.) South-Western Cengage Learning, retrieved from academic.cengage.com
5. Bryce, T. (2006). *Individualism vs. teamwork*. Retrieved from http://www.articles base.com/corporate-articles/individualism-vs-teamwork-32264.html
6. Kaipa, P., Chowdary, S. & Jagadeesh, B. V. (2009). *Soft skills are smart skills*. Retrieved from http://selfcorp.prasadkaipa.com/selfcorpnew/softskillsV6.pdf
7. Kaipa, P., et al.
8. Maslow, A. H. (1996). *The psychology of science: A reconnaissance*. New York, NY: Harper & Row.
9. Bennis W., & Goldsmith, J. (2003). *Learning to lead*. New York, NY: Perseus Books Group.

Inner-Self Competency

What You Bring to a Team Environment

As you become more clear about who you really are, you'll be better able to decide what is best for you—the first time around.

—Oprah Winfrey

Introduction

The focus of Chapter 2 is on the individual's relationship with the world as illustrated in the following diagram. This chapter explores the importance of self-awareness first, followed by self-development as tools for success in personal, social and work-related activities. As you move from chapter to chapter, it is important to use the information from previous chapters as stepping stones to learning and developing additional knowledge, skills and abilities.

Who are you? Is this a simple, straightforward question or a complex inquiry? How would a good friend describe you? What about your family, your spouse, your boss, your in-laws or your neighbors and coworkers; how would any of them describe you? In the context of working well with others, experts associate interpersonal skills with the individual's knowledge, skills and abilities that are developed to interact well with others. How do you describe yourself? Do you have the skill set to develop and use the interpersonal skills needed to work well with others?

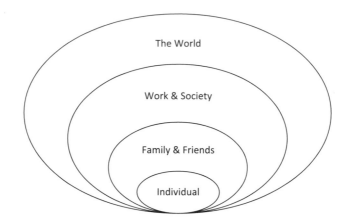

Figure 2.1

Chapter 2 Competencies

The purpose of this chapter is to help you:

- Apply concepts of self-development to the teamwork environment.
- Practice techniques suitable for learning through self-reflection.
- Review personality theory in the context of teamwork.
- Apply personality theory concepts to ongoing self-development practices.

Before moving on to other aspects of the environment in other chapters, let's begin with the individual. Back to the initial question: Who are you? First, the question must be placed in the proper context. Individuals have varying levels of knowledge, skills and abilities. Each learning experience has a cumulative effect on the competencies needed for effective group or team engagement. It is important to realize that the individuals who participate in a group/team might be at different readiness levels than those needed to achieve a common goal. The expectations set by the need to create the group do not always meet the group's ability to perform as a team. The first step for raising individual competency levels is to explore the area of self-awareness.

There are many ways in which a person can learn about himself or herself. Some of the most effective ways include self-reflection, feedback from others, open mindedness and self-awareness.[1] Learning activities include everything from formal educational experiences to self-development activities. Most formal educational experiences are structured and instructor led, while

Figure 2.2

self-development activities are informal and self-directed. An individual can achieve maximum results from combining both types of learning.

Learning is something everyone does on a daily basis. Some individuals seem to absorb new information more readily than others, and the reasons for this are the subject of years of research. One study reports that only 14% of learning occurs in the classroom during a given year, and suggests that 53% of an individual's time is spent in community and home activities. The remaining 33% of the time is spent sleeping.[2] The patterns observed in this study certainly support the notion that much of our learning experiences occur outside of the formal classroom.

Self-Reflection

During a panel discussion held at the Kellogg School of Management of Northwestern University, Clinical Professor Harry Kraemer defined self-reflection as "the process of silencing the noise and identifying goals."[3] Visually, self-reflection is like picking up a camera, pointing it at yourself and taking a picture; a self-portrait. The key to effective self-reflection is the thought process that occurs after taking the self-portrait. It is about taking a past experience, thinking about it, assessing the pros and cons, and making a choice about how to approach future experiences.

Self-reflection can be overwhelming if more than one question is considered in one session. Simplification is important and can be achieved by taking one question at a time. The purpose of self reflection is to achieve quality results, one step at a time; to do one thing well is usually more beneficial than to do many things badly.

Exercise: Self-Reflection—Step 1

Some people like to write in a journal while others prefer other methods of self-reflection. The method does not matter. What matters is finding a comfortable way to learn this valuable set of skills or competency. One way to start is to think about a task that must be completed today, and assess the success or failure to accomplish that task.

There is no right or wrong response to the question or statements in this exercise. The goal is to take some time to conduct a mental series of steps for reflection after or before a routine day.

Table 2.1 Example: Specific Task

Task (Topic)	Action	Reflection (What did you learn?)
Plan a family reunion: determine size of planning committee.	Contacted 5 family members.	Family members want to attend the reunion, yet have no time to help with the plans.
	Contacted 5 additional family members.	Found 2 who can help plan the event.
	Asked each family member who can help to contact 5 additional family members.	Continue with this process until a planning committee forms.
	Start the plans.	A family reunion requires planning and time. This is a tremendous amount of work for one individual. Working with a group helps to distribute the work to accomplish a common goal.

Table 2.2 Example: General Self-Reflection

Topic	Action	Reflection (What did you learn?)
Self-assessment	Write down 5 things that you like about yourself.	1 I like to learn about new points of view.
		2 I like to relax and have fun.
		3 I have a good sense of humor.
		4 I am kind.
		5 I am open-minded.

The template used in the previous example is simple by design. Select one task, question or statement at a time to avoid confusion, as this helps to practice the skill of self-reflection. Approach each attempt as a brainstorming exercise without criticism or judgment; just the facts. Keep a written record of the exercises for future review and reflection.

Practice

Use the same template from the example for the following suggested exercise comments. Consider the following examples[4] for the practice sessions or create your own comments. Remember to take one item at a time for best results.

Consider the Following Examples

1   Once a week, write down three kind things that were done for you. Also, write down three things you did for someone else.
2   Think of a person or persons who have really made a difference in your life.
3   List at least four things that you do well.
4   Write down five things that you like about yourself.
5   Think of three authors, artists or musicians who have inspired you or whose work you have simply enjoyed. Make a promise to yourself to read, view or listen to their work again soon.
6   Remember a time when you felt supported and nurtured in an hour of need. Describe this time and how you felt.
7   Remember three times when you felt inner peace and serenity. As you recapture the feeling, write it down.
8   What obstacles have you overcome recently? Thank yourself and those who helped you.
9   Think of someone you might forgive and how that might change your life.

10 With whom do you laugh the most? Remember a time you laughed so hard, you thought you would collapse.

11 Remember a wonderful place you have visited and how it made you feel.

12 What is your favorite thing to do? How does it make you feel?

13 Think of one quality that you would like to work on that could increase your potential for most of your activities (e.g., patience, compassion, kindness, empathy).

14 If you were to leave this life tomorrow, what would you want people to remember about you?

15 Write down a list of things for which you are thankful. Add to it every day, and share your list with others.

The previous questions are steps in a process. This is not an isolated assignment; set a date in a calendar to remind you to revisit this list on a regular basis, one question at a time. This is only one step in the journey of getting to know more about your inner self. Make it a priority to review your questions and answers. Try to share your answers with others; perhaps, begin with someone you truly trust and expand from there.

Exercise: Self-Reflection—Step 2

What you learn from answering self-reflection questions, such as the ones you just answered, is merely a warm-up exercise. The next crucial step is to determine, more specifically, how you have learned valuable lessons to date. How do you deal with failure? What mistakes have you made, and what did you learn from those mistakes? Are you making "smarter mistakes" as a result of what you have learned? In other words, are you repeating old mistakes or making new ones?

Example: The Valuable Results of Making Mistakes

First, briefly answer the following questions:

1 What were you taught, in your youth, about mistakes? *To get it right the first time.*

2 Can you think of an example when you made a mistake? *I failed to complete chores.*

3 How did the influential people in your life react? *They were disappointed.*

4 How were you treated? *I was given more chores as a punishment.*

5 How did you feel? *Like a failure.*

Next, use the stated answers to answer the following questions:

1   What did you do in the past? *I made a choice that led to a mistake.*
2   What did you learn? *That I could avoid the mistake by making a different choice.*
3   What can you do in the future? *Make better choices.*

Finally, apply the following six steps to your decision-making process. Use the chart provided for each exercise/practice:

1   Think about it: Take one item at a time.
2   Write it down: Keep it simple. Perhaps you enjoy keeping a journal. If not, then make it a habit to write notes in a regular place and on a regular basis.
3   Research/feedback: Read about what others have done or ask someone for their thoughts.
4   Possibilities: Make a list of possible solutions to your dilemma or situation.
5   Action: Select one approach and take action.
6   Reflection: How did it work out? Think about what went well and what needs work. Repeat as necessary.

Table 2.3 Chart for Exercise/Practice

Past Behavior	Future Behavior	Six-Step Process
Made a choice that led to a mistake.	Make a smarter choice.	1 Think about it.
		2 Write it down: I answered the questions listed above.
		3 Research/feedback: Talked to those in charge and peers.
		4 Possibilities: * repeat choice * make a smarter choice * do nothing
		5 Action: * make a smarter choice
		6 Reflection * What happened? * What went well? * What needs work?

Practice with the following questions, or write your own questions.

1 As a young adult, perhaps while attending school or during your first job, what were your experiences regarding mistakes? Write an example of a specific situation. What happened? How did your educators or supervisors react? How were you treated? How did you feel?

2 Think of a more recent experience during which you made a mistake, and write it down. What happened? How did others to whom you report react? How were you treated? How did you feel?

3 Do you recognize any patterns in your answers to the previous questions?

4 How do you react to the mistakes or failures of others?

5 Do you recognize any patterns in your reactions to how you have been treated after making a mistake and how you treat others when they make mistakes?

6 What do you want instead? Identify one behavior or reaction that you would like to improve.

Next, use the answers from the practice questions to answer the following questions:

1 What did you do in the past? _____

2 What did you learn? _____

3 What can you do in the future? _____

Finally, apply the six steps to your decision-making process. Use the chart provided to write your goal and how you plan to achieve it.

Table 2.4 Chart for Exercise:

Past Behavior	Future Behavior (Goal)	Plan
		1 Think about it.
		2 Write it down.
		3 Research/feedback
		4 Possibilities
		5 Action
		6 Reflection

Six-Step Instructions

1   Think about it: Take one item at a time.
2   Write it down: Keep it simple. Perhaps you enjoy keeping a journal. If not, then make it a habit to write notes in a regular place and on a regular basis.
3   Research/feedback: Read about what others have done or ask someone for their thoughts.
4   Possibilities: Make a list of possible solutions to your dilemma or opportunity.
5   Action: Select one approach and take action.
6   Reflection: How did it work out? Think about what went well and what needs work, and repeat as necessary.

Exercise Recap

Some individuals can go through a self-reflection exercise without hesitation, while others will struggle and find the process difficult. Whether you complete exercises like those in this book easily or not depends on several factors: style, experience, education, exposure and so on. Exposure to self-development activities can occur at home, at work, at school, at church or at a social event, to name a few of the possibilities. Self-assessment tests are bountiful and can be quite useful. Individuals involved with large organizations (schools and employers) usually have easy access to such tools as self-assessments. Together with training and education, self-assessments can provide valuable insight into an individual's knowledge, skills and abilities. In his *Self-Assessment Library,* Robbins states, "The *Self-Assessment Library* has been created to help you to learn more about yourself so that you might become 'enlightened'. It draws on numerous instruments that have been developed by behavioral researchers that tap into your skills, abilities, and interests".[5] Theory and practice in the field of self-development asserts that the value of these activities is strongly correlated to successful interactions with others. Successful interactions with others are strongly correlated to improved performance.

Hellriegel and Slocum describe self-knowledge in terms of a competency; a self-competency. They define a self-competency as the "knowledge, skills, and abilities to assess personal strengths and weaknesses, set and pursue professional and personal goals, balance work and personal life, and engage in new learning."[6] Self-knowledge, self-awareness and self-competency are only a few ways of describing the opportunity of knowing oneself better in a systematic way; as tools for improved business relationships. The theory and practice of developing self-knowledge might seem common sense to some; nevertheless, it is a lost opportunity to many. Behavioral research consistently supports the positive relationship between individual competencies and behavior in general. These relationships are at the core of what happens when people work in groups or teams. Self-knowledge is critical because of the relationships between the individual, family/friends, work/society and the world. Self-development that occurs in tandem with these other entities tends to spill over into developing other competencies as well. The common factor that weaves throughout the relationships described above is behavior, and behavioral researchers tie personality and behavior to characteristics that support productivity in teams.

Personality

Personality is the one word that describes what makes an individual unique. An individual's personality also describes what a person has in common with others as well as what makes that person different. Behavioral researchers tend to agree that personality, while the result of many contributing variables is usually affected the most by two primary influences. About half of personality traits are inherited from the genetic makeup of family characteristics. The other half of personality traits are developed through life experiences.[7]

Organizations are well known for using personality tests to assess an employee's personality traits and attitudes during the hiring process, promotions and when assigning individuals to teams and workgroups. Two of the most frequently used instruments are the *Minnesota Multiphasic Personality Inventory* (MMPI) and the *Myers-Briggs Type Indicator* (MBTI). These assessments identify behaviors that help employers determine relationships between personality and competencies in the work environment.[8] Another important contributor to the study of individual characteristics is psychologist Daniel Goleman; he introduced the concept of emotional intelligence (EI). In spite of criticisms about the reliability and validity of Goleman's research, organizations are increasingly paying attention to EI because of the correlations between Goleman's research and career success. More specifically, EI refers to an individual's ability to handle interpersonal relationships. The areas of interest included in EI include self-awareness, social empathy, self-motivation and social skills.[9] While technical skills can be determined by a variety of assessments, determination of interpersonal skills remains a challenge.

Behavioral and organizational research, in a literature review of studies conducted during the past 20 years, proposes that the numerous personality traits of individuals fall into five primary dimensions. The dimensions are commonly referred to as the Big Five. Gibson et al. describe the Big Five personality dimensions:[10]

- Conscientiousness—Is an individual dependable and hardworking?
- Extraversion–introversion—Is an individual sociable or reserved?
- Agreeableness—Does an individual work well with others?
- Emotional stability—How well does an individual handle stress?
- Openness to experience—To what degree does an individual have an interest in new experiences?

Exercise: Personality Traits

The following list includes traits associated with each of the Big Five personality dimensions. Review the list and identify the traits with which you identify the most.

Table 2.5

Personality Dimension	Personality traits of individuals who tend to be more open to opportunities.	Personality traits of individuals who tend to be less open to opportunities.
Conscientiousness	• Dependable • Hardworking • Organized • Thorough • Persistent	• Distracted • Unmotivated • Unorganized • Inattentive to detail • Gives up easily
Extraversion–introversion	• Sociable • Outgoing • Assertive • Active • Talkative	• Loner • Shy • Passive • Inactive • Quiet
Agreeableness	• Friendly • Cooperative • Flexible • Trusting • Tolerant	• Reserved • Guarded • Inflexible • Cautious • Judgmental

(Continued)

Table 2.5 (Continued)

Personality Dimension	Personality traits of individuals who tend to be more open to opportunities.	Personality traits of individuals who tend to be less open to opportunities.
Emotional stability	• Consistent • Think before reacting • Generally calm • Positive attitude • Can manage my anger	• Inconsistent • Impulsive • Anxious • Insecure • Angers easily
Openness to experience	• Like learning new things • Like meeting new people • Like going to new places • Curious • Imaginative	• Like what is known • Like status quo • Like known places • Lack curiosity • Like reality

Example: Here is the same chart with an added section inserted after each personality dimension. Read each example situation at the end of each personality dimension and describe how you might handle the circumstances. Each section includes one example response for individuals who tend to be more open to new opportunities and one example for individuals who tend to be less open to opportunities. There is no right or wrong response. The responses are merely indicators of the personality traits with which you identify and find more comfortable.

Table 2.6

Personality Dimension	Personality traits of individuals who tend to be more open to new opportunities.	Personality traits of individuals who tend to be less open to opportunities.
Conscientiousness	• Dependable • Hardworking • Organized • Thorough • Persistent	• Distracted • Unmotivated • Unorganized • Inattentive to detail • Gives up easily

Table 2.6 (Continued)

Personality Dimension	Personality traits of individuals who tend to be more open to new opportunities.	Personality traits of individuals who tend to be less open to opportunities.
Example scenario: The coming weekend marks the date for you to use your tickets for a special event that you planned months ago. The phone rings, and it is your boss who asks you to work this weekend.		
Response (more open to opportunities): You tell your boss that you will see her this weekend and make other arrangements for the tickets.		
Response (less open to opportunities): You tell your boss that you cannot work this weekend and you attend the special event.		
Extraversion– introversion	• Sociable • Outgoing • Assertive • Active • Talkative	• Loner • Shy • Passive • Inactive • Quiet
Example scenario: After a difficult week, a friend calls you to invite you to a special event.		
Response (more open to opportunities): You are excited about the invitation and agree to attend it with your friend.		
Response (less open to opportunities): You thank your friend, and you pass on the invitation to spend some quiet time alone.		
Agreeableness	• Friendly • Cooperative • Flexible • Trusting • Tolerant	• Reserved • Guarded • Inflexible • Cautious • Judgmental
Example scenario: Your closest friend who lives in another city had planned to visit you for the weekend. At the last minute he calls you to change the visit to another weekend.		
Response (more open to opportunities): You tell him it is no problem to change the plans, and you compare calendars to set a future date for the visit.		
Response (less open to opportunities): You are upset with your friend; cannot believe that he wants to change plans at the last minute.		
Emotional stability	• Consistent • Think before reacting • Generally calm • Positive attitude • Can manage my anger	• Inconsistent • Impulsive • Anxious • Insecure • Angers easily

(Continued)

Table 2.6 (Continued)

Personality Dimension	Personality traits of individuals who tend to be more open to new opportunities.	Personality traits of individuals who tend to be less open to opportunities.
Example scenario: You are driving on the freeway and another driver pulls in front of you. Response (more open to opportunities): You pull back from the driver and continue on with your drive. Response (less open to opportunities): You speed up and pass the driver.		
Openness to experience	• Like learning new things • Like meeting new people • Like going to new places • Curious • Imaginative	• Like what is known • Like status quo • Like known places • Lack curiosity • Like reality
Example scenario: Instead of going to the same restaurant for lunch, a coworker suggests a newly opened restaurant. Response (more open to opportunities): You want to know all about it and cannot wait to try the new restaurant. Response (less open to opportunities): You would rather go to the familiar restaurant.		

Practice

Now, use the following chart to practice. The following list includes traits associated with each of the Big Five personality dimensions. Review the list and identify the traits with which you identify the most. This time, write your own scenario for each personality dimension.

Table 2.7

Personality Dimension	Personality traits of individuals who tend to be more open to opportunities.	Personality traits of individuals who tend to be less open to opportunities.
Conscientiousness	• Dependable • Hardworking • Organized • Thorough • Persistent	• Distracted • Unmotivated • Unorganized • Inattentive to detail • Gives up easily

Personality Dimension	Personality traits of individuals who tend to be more open to opportunities.	Personality traits of individuals who tend to be less open to opportunities.
Extraversion–introversion	• Sociable • Outgoing • Assertive • Active • Talkative	• Loner • Shy • Passive • Inactive • Quiet
Agreeablencss	• Friendly • Cooperative • Flexible • Trusting • Tolerant	• Reserved • Guarded • Inflexible • Cautious • Judgmental
Emotional stability	• Consistent • Think before reacting • Generally calm • Positive attitude • Can manage my anger	• Inconsistent • Impulsive • Anxious • Insecure • Angers easily
Openness to experience	• Like learning new things • Like meeting new people • Like going to new places • Curious • Imaginative	• Like what is known • Like status quo • Like known places • Lack curiosity • Like reality

Exercise Recap

Studies in this field continue to reveal findings which support the relationships between the Big Five personality dimensions and successful behavior in the work environment.[11] The individual is the foundation for self development. It is within the individual's control to iteratively learn and apply new information throughout the other "arenas" of life: family & friends, work & society and globally.

What about you? Are you easy or difficult to work with? The MBTI is the most widely used assessment of personality type in the world.[12] Decades of research shed remarkable information on the use and application of the MBTI in the context of working in groups/teams. Individuals, human beings, come with unique sets of preferences in how they energize, gather information, make decisions and view life.[13] The following chart describes the basic premise for the MBTI.[14]

E Extraversion _____	Introversion	**I**
(Energized by outer world)	(Energized by inner world)	
S Sensing _____	Intuition	**N**
(Work with known facts)	(Look for possibilities and meanings)	
T Thinking _____	Feeling	**F**
(Base decisions on objective analysis)	(Base decisions on personal values)	
J Judgment _____	Perception	**P**
(Prefer a planned, decided way of life)	(Prefer a flexible, spontaneous way of life)	

Study and analyze your traits, characteristics, and preferences because these individual attributes become contributing factors to the success or failure of an individual and of a team/group. Successful group work depends on factors such as balanced skill sets, a common purpose, specific goals, accountability and reliability. On the other end of the continuum of success, many groups/teams fail to achieve their goals because of infighting, lack of trust and lack of necessary skills. The common element in each of the outcomes is the ability of an individual to know, understand and develop individual interpersonal skills or competencies. Isabel Briggs Myers, one of the researchers who created the MBTI, said it best:

> When people differ, a knowledge of type lessens friction and eases strain. In addition, it reveals *the value of differences*. No one has to be good at everything. By developing individual strengths, guarding against known weaknesses, and appreciating the strengths of the other types, life will be more amusing, more interesting, and more of a daily adventure than it could possibly be if everyone were alike.[15]

Attitude

The individual's attitude is an additional important concept in the discussion of interpersonal skill development. Attitudes are the visible expressions, the evidence, of an individual's thoughts, feelings and behaviors.

A study about the effectiveness of work groups and teams by Kozlowski and Llgen clearly supports the value of pursuing proficient levels of interpersonal skills. The study's findings elaborate on the western world's focus on individual development while most work environments depend on the work of teams and groups. While schools educate individuals and corporations employ individuals, these same individuals are then assigned to teams with high expectations for their success. At the same time, little is formally done to enhance team training, development and leadership.[16] Many research studies exist that provide processes that help individuals to combine their knowledge, skills and abilities with others to produce successful teams.

While there is evidence that individual competencies can influence team effectiveness, and that these competencies can be learned, the current educational structure must catch up with the needs of our organizations and institutions.[17] Hence, the value of self-development becomes increasingly important.

Summary of Concepts

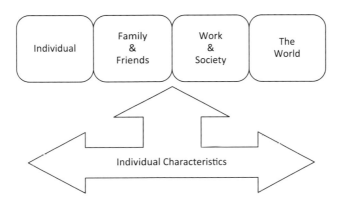

Figure 2.3

In this chapter, we continued emphasizing the individual's characteristics, which we began in Chapter 1. The purpose of Chapter 1 and Chapter 2 is to establish a foundation upon which to build additional layers of connectivity and relationships between the individual and effective group- and teamwork. Just as an individual's strengths and weaknesses develop over time, so does the effectiveness of a group or team.

Chapter 3 further develops the individual's strengths and weaknesses in the context of a diversity competency: What you need to know about today's workforce. Today's work environment is undeniably complex, on many levels. The content of Chapter 3 will add another layer of complexity to the individual's perspective regarding effective inclusion in group and team activities.

Review Questions

1 Discuss the importance of self-development as it relates to teamwork.
2 Discuss useful techniques for learning through self-reflection.
3 What role does an individual's personality play in the team environment?
4 Discuss the role of personality theory concepts in ongoing self-development practices.

Note: Answers to the review questions are located in the Appendix.

Notes

* Winfrey, O. (2013). The Biography Channel Web site. Retrieved from http://www.biography.com/people/oprah-winfrey-9534419

1. Bennis, W., & Goldsmith, J. (2003). *Learning to lead* (3rd ed.). New York, NY: Perseus Books Group.
2. Bransford, J. (2000). *How people learn: Brain, mind, experience and school.* Washington, DC: National Academy Press.
3. Smith, D. P. (2011). Clinical Professor Harry Kraemer's panel discussion on the four principles of values-based leadership. Retrieved 05/22/2011 from http://www.kellogg.northwestern.edu/News_Articles/2011/self-reflection.aspx
4. Adapted from My First Joy Journal, by Loretta LaRoche, 1998, in *Relax—You may only have a few minutes left.* New York: Random House,.
5. Robbins, S. P. (2009). Self-assessment library (Version 3.4, p. vi). Upper Saddle River, NJ: Pearson/Prentice Hall.
6. Hellriegel, D., & Slocum, J. W. *Organizational behavior* (13th ed.). Mason, OH: South-Western Cengage Learning.
7. Hellriegel & Slocum.
8. Gibson, J., Ivancevich, J. M., Donnelly, J. H. & Konopaske, R. (2012). *Organizations* (14th ed.). New York, NY: McGraw-Hill Irwin.
9. Hellriegel & Slocum; Gibson, et al.
10. Gibson, J. L., et. al.
11. Bozionelos, N. (2004). The Big Five of personality and work involvement. *Journal of Managerial Psychology, 19,* 69–81.
12. Myers & Briggs Foundation. MBTI Basics.
13. Robbins, S. P. & Hunsaker, P. L. (2012). Training in interpersonal skills (6th ed.). Boston, MA: Prentice Hall.
14. Kummerow, J. M. (1997). Center for Applications of Psychological Type.
15. Lawrence, G. (1993). People types and tiger stripes (3rd ed.). Center for Application of Psychological Type, Inc. 1993. (Introduction to Type by Isabel Briggs

Myers is included in this volume by permission of Consulting Psychologists Press. Copyright 1976 by Isabel Briggs Myers, p. 225.)

16. Kozlowski, S. W. J., & Llgen, D. R. (2006). Enhancing the effectiveness of work groups and teams. *Psychological Science in the Public Interest, 7*, 77–124.

17. Kozlowski, S. W. J., & Llgen, D. R. (2006). Enhancing the effectiveness of work groups and teams. *Psychological Science in the Public Interest, 7*, 77–124.

Diversity Competency

What You Need to Know About Today's Workforce

We have become not a melting pot but a beautiful mosaic. Different people, different beliefs, different yearnings, different hopes, different dreams.

—Jimmy Carter

Introduction

Chapter 2 highlighted the individual's role in various aspects of life, such as work, social events and family activities. The intent, in Chapter 2, was to turn the focus internally in an attempt to bring an individual to a self-reflective state of mind. While the context and the common thread throughout this textbook are about working in groups, it is always important to begin by understanding ourselves first.

In Chapter 3, the focus quickly turns outward to those around us. We seem to readily know how diverse the world around us has become; yet, the challenge remains in how we should honor our differences and leverage the new found strengths toward increased productivity.

Our world of work is more diverse than ever in our history. Some of the changes that have impacted our environment include changes in the characteristics of the population such as age, gender, race, ethnicity, sexual orientation and mental/physical abilities. In order to define diversity, Chapter 3

Chapter 3 Competencies

The Purpose of this chapter is to help you:

• Describe seven types of stereotypes found in today's work environment.

• Apply available resources that can be used to promote inclusion.

• Explain the relationship between personality and diversity in the workplace.

Figure 3.1

includes information about how diversity has evolved throughout history in society and in the work environment. An individual can improve relationships with others by learning about diversity and, most important, to value diversity in the context of productivity through working effectively with others in a group or team setting.

Diversity initiatives date back to the 1960s, during a time when discrimination was rampant. Many of the initiatives which were supported by organizations were driven by the civil rights movement. Data gathered over time began to correlate the results of diversity programs with increased productivity in the work environment. Although current research validates the increase in diversity awareness in organizations, the actual impact of a deeper understanding of differences between individuals remains the subject of many studies.[1] Awareness of diversity, the benefits of diversity and the issues that arise in a diverse work environment is the first and easiest step. The real challenge lies in honoring individual differences in order to leverage the differences for increased productivity and the development of relationships in our environment. Bell, Villado, Lukasik, Belau and Briggs in their meta-analysis of diversity research concluded their study by stating, "Although team diversity research is thriving, unclear results and mixed conclusions are pervasive. We believe that the lack of clarity may be attributed to a consistent oversimplification of diversity."[2]

Stereotypes

Stereotypes generalize certain characteristics of a group, and generalizations negate individual differences. Generally, when stereotyping occurs, some type of discrimination follows, and the diversity within groups goes without further discovery. Avoid making assumptions about how those different from you will act in a given situation. When you trust your and other's good intentions, you remain open to learning about different practices and customs. Just because someone is different, it does not make them wrong or inferior. Plan to notice how those from different cultures conduct their business so that you can collaborate with them to discover new and perhaps improved processes and applications of common areas. The first step is to learn about some of the most common components of our diverse world. What follows are some key concepts in taking a step toward understanding and honoring diversity.

Diversity Defined

Diversity, in our current environment, has a much broader definition than ever before. Basically, diversity defines those characteristics that make individuals different from one another. Traditional models of diversity include characteristics that the individual is born with, and these characteristics are usually visible. The traditional model includes race, gender, age and physical ability. The broader, inclusion model of diversity includes dimensions of individual differences that might be acquired over time or change over time. Successful leaders of organizations tend to view diversity in terms of doing what is necessary to support the broadest range of individual differences.[3]

Table 3.1 Examples of Traditional and Inclusive Diversity Models

Traditional Diversity Model	Inclusive Diversity Model
• Race	• Race—ethnic group
• Age	• Age—stage of development
• Gender	• Gender—sexual characteristics
• Physical ability	• Physical Ability—bodily strength
	• Sexual orientation—other than heterosexuality
	• Military experience—spent time in the military service
	• Personality set of individual characteristics

Awareness Exercise: How do you define diversity? Following are some suggested definitions of diversity. Add your own definition in the space provided. Also, write a brief description or the name of someone you know who matches this diversity characteristic. The purpose of this exercise is to raise awareness of the diverse people in your social and work environments.

Table 3.2

Inclusive Diversity Model	Additional Definition	I Know Someone
• Race—ethnic group		
• Age—stage of development		
• Gender—sexual characteristics		
• Physical ability—bodily strength		
• Sexual orientation—other than heterosexuality		
• Military experience—spent time in the military service		
• Personality—set of individual characteristics		

Awareness Exercise Reflection

Take time to review your Awareness Exercise chart periodically. One of the benefits of completing this exercise and reviewing your comments is to determine if your group or team environment is serving the purpose for which it was created. Having the best individuals in your group or team can and often does determine the group's success in achieving common goals.

While there is no right or wrong answer to the Awareness Exercise, it is beneficial to make wiser decisions based on the knowledge of critical information. The Awareness Exercise includes only a few examples of the growing list of inclusive categories. Working with individuals who are similar to us can be difficult enough, and working with those who are different can be even more difficult. It is wise to be prepared.

Diversity in the Workplace

Some of the most compelling reasons for including members of diverse groups in work teams include:[4]

- Additional talent in the work environment.
- Creative approaches to problem solving.
- Improved decision making.
- Competitive advantage due to a larger pool of talent.

Some of the challenges of diversity include:

- The need to focus on the organization's or team's common interest (goal).
- Deciding how much diversity is right.
- Diverse teams sometimes experience more conflict.
- Solo members of representative groups may feel stereotyped.

Dealing With Diversity: Concepts You Need to Know About Each Diversity Dimension

Race—Ethnic Group

Who Are They?

According to the Center for Immigration Studies, as of March 2007, Mexico serves as the largest immigration source country of newcomers to the United States. Mexican immigrants account for six times as many immigrants as the next largest country, China. China's immigrants include people from

Taiwan and Hong Kong. Other significant sources of immigrants include Latin American and Caribbean countries. One of the interesting findings about contemporary immigration research is that there has been a significant decline in the diversity of immigrants: "Mexico accounts for 31 percent of all immigrants in 2007, up from 28 percent in 2000, 22 percent in 1990, and 16 percent in 1980. The top sending country in 1970 was Italy, which accounted for only 10 percent of the foreign-born."[5]

In addition to immigrants, there are numerous other visitors who enter the United States under temporary visas. Temporary visas allow visitors who do not wish to immigrate to the United States permission to remain on a temporary basis for reasons ranging from academic pursuits to vacations. There are over 30 different types of visas available for visitors. The United States issued almost 500,000 visas in 2010. Another 55,000 visas are issued on a yearly basis through a congressionally mandated Diversity Immigrant Visa Program. Diversity visas are drawn from random selection to persons who meet the requirements and submit applications. These visas are designed to attract immigrants from countries with low rates of immigration to the United States.[6]

Common Stereotypes[7]

- African Americans excel in sports.
- African Americans are involved in crime and violence.
- Asians are good at math.
- Asians know martial arts.
- Jews are rich.
- Jews have crooked noses.
- Latinos are all immigrants.
- Latinos are all Mexican.
- Middle Easterners hate America.
- Middle Easterners, Islamics and Arabs are all the same.
- Native Americans are lazy.
- Native Americans are alcoholics.

Inclusion Tips and Resources

- Seek out information by conducting research.
- Join culturally diverse groups.
- Ask questions from legitimate sources.

- Organizations that have information:
  - http://www.aclu.org (American Civil Liberties Union)
  - http://www.now.org (National Organization of Women)
  - www.urban.org (The Urban League)
  - www.usa.gov (List of Federal Agencies)

Age—Stage of Development

Who Are They?

The 2010 U.S. Census report breaks down the total population of 308,745,539 people into the following age groups:

- Under 18 years of age—74,181,467
- 18 to 44 years of age—112,806,642
- 45 to 64 years of age—81,489,445
- 65 years and over—40,267,984[8]

The significance of the numbers by age groups is the phenomenon that these groups have created in our current work environment. For the first time in U.S. history, there are four generations working side by side. What used to be called a "generation gap" is now referred to as "generational differences." Working with individuals from different generations means working with different sets of values, expectations, attitudes, styles of communication and views, to name a few. The four generations are commonly referred to as the traditional generation, the baby boom generation, generation X and generation Y. Highlights of each generation's characteristics are listed in the following chart.[9]

Although the chart contains distinct lines between the generations, there are many overlaps, depending on the source of the information. What is important to take away from this information is that individuals from these generations come with identifiable differences in the way they think, behave, are motivated and in what they value. Knowing more about the differences can be a valuable tool for increased success in working with groups and teams.

Common Stereotypes

- Older workers are less motivated than younger workers.
- Older workers are less productive than younger workers.
- Older workers are more resistant to change.
- Older workers are harder to train.

Table 3.3

Characteristics	Traditional	Baby Boomers	Generation X	Generation Y
Age group	Born 1922–1945	Born 1946–1964	Born 1963–1982	Born 1980–2002
Influenced by	Great Depression World War II	Vietnam War Civil Rights Kennedy & King assassinations Watergate Sexual revolution	MTV AIDS Worldwide competition Computer and video games Latchkey kids	Excess Computers Technological advances
Mostly known for	Conservative Disciplined Formal Respect Authority	Liberal Sense of entitlement Optimistic Avoid conflict Change oriented "Show me" generation	Ambitious Work & life balance Independent Self-reliant Value continuous learning Adaptable to change	Embrace diversity Optimistic Like change Seek flexibility
Work attitude	Loyal workers Dedicated Non-risk takers Team players Collaborative Prefer order Hardworking	Seek job security Workaholics Team players Collaborative Value chain of command	Want instant feedback Not loyal to employers Strong technical skills Results focused Like flexible schedules Entrepreneurial Labeled "slackers"	Multitaskers Value teamwork Highly educated Value training Confident Entrepreneurial Results focused
Social status	Communicate well Affluent	Accept diversity Value health and wellness Value personal growth Value personal gratification	Loyal to friends Individualistic Like diversity Work & life balance	Demanding Embrace diversity Work & life balance

- Older workers have less ability to learn.
- Older workers cost more due to higher wages and benefits.
- Younger workers are not as dependable, honest or trustworthy.
- Younger workers are not as loyal to the job.
- Younger workers are more likely to create turnover problems.
- Younger workers are healthier and more productive.
- Younger workers are more energetic and more productive.
- Younger workers provide higher return on investment.[10]

Inclusion Tips and Resources

- Continuous learning about generational differences.
- Constant vigilance of common stereotypes.
- Seek out individuals from different age groups in social and business environments.
- Organizations that have information:
  - www.urban.org (The Urban League)
  - www.usa.gov (List of Federal Agencies)

Gender—Sexual Characteristics

Who Are They?

According to the 2010 U.S. Census, 49.2% of the population is male and 50.8% of the population is female.[11] These data are mainly based on the primary difference between males and females: sexual organs. The research on gender differences is substantial, so the purpose of the following section is to briefly provide some general information in the context of working well with others.

Gender-role theory and social-role theory provide a wide background for understanding the views of the differences between men and women. Gender-role theory supports the notion that men and women learn the behavior that is expected from them by the family and culture in which they developed from their birth. Gender-role theory includes the belief that non-physical attributes to gender are learned through socialization.[12]

Social-role theory is about males and females acquiring their differences through their roles in society. Patterns of social behavior, based on the cultural norms set by society, tend to perpetuate gender types of behavior. The repetitive cycle that supports and encourages social role is also responsible for some of the stereotypes that have developed over time.[13]

Common Stereotypes

Typical stereotypes of males and females include the following:

Table 3.4

Typical Male Stereotypes	Typical Female Stereotypes
• Men do not listen	• Women talk too much
• Men do not ask for directions	• Women cannot drive
• Men do not talk about feelings	• Women love talking about feelings
• Men do not get emotional	• Women are emotional
• Men separate personal and work life	• Women talk about personal life at work
• Men are more aggressive	• Aggressive women act like men
• Men are more physical/strong	• Women cannot handle physical activities
• Men like sports	• Women do not like sports
• Men are tough	• Women are more nurturing
• Men do not like to shop	• Women like to shop
• Men are not fashion oriented	• Women are more fashion oriented
• Men want sex	• Women want conversation
• Men excel at math/science	• Women excel in literature/art
• Men cannot cook	• Women can cook
• Men are better leaders/managers	• Women cannot lead/manage
• Men do not cry	• Women cry easily

The stereotypes listed are only a few examples of prevailing notions that exist in contemporary social and work environments. Exceptions do exist in each category. Some notable exceptions include politicians who cry in public (Stereotype: Men do not cry), and women political leaders (Stereotype: Men are better leaders). Political figures, both male and female, in the 21st century, have shattered some of the most longstanding stereotypes. Although stereotypes and exceptions to the stereotypes have existed for centuries, it seems that the exceptions are now receiving more media exposure. The purpose of the list is to raise awareness so that individuals do not continue to promote stereotypes and avoid adding more to the list.

Inclusion Tips and Resources

- Become an avid reader of information from all sources.
- Avoid perpetuating stereotypes by speaking up.
- Socialize and conduct business with individuals of both genders.

- Organizations that have information:
  - www.usa.gov (List of Federal Agencies)

Physical Ability—Bodily Strength

Who Are They?

Physical ability is generally defined as an individual's ability to efficiently and effectively complete physical tasks. Individuals share an array of both temporary and permanent physical disabilities that might hinder their ability to perform certain tasks. Yet, individuals with impaired physical abilities are still viable members of groups and teams. Awareness of variances in physical abilities helps group members overcome biases that create counterproductive stereotypes among group members.

According to the Center for Disease Control and the U.S. Census Bureau reports, the most common disability in the United States is arthritis or rheumatism. The aging population of the baby boomer generation is a significant contributor to the incidence of arthritis. Other causes of physical disability include spine problems and heart trouble. Further analysis of reports by the CDC and the Census Bureau indicate that women show much higher numbers of disability factors than men at all ages. As large numbers of the baby boomer generation reach the age of 65, these numbers are expected to rise.

The CDC conducted a longitudinal study, Survey of Income and Program Participation, during 2004–2005 to determine the significance of disabilities in the U.S. population. One yes answer to any of the following questions indicated that a person suffered from a physical disability:

1 Use of an assistive aid (cane, crutches, walker, or wheelchair);
2 Difficulty performing activities of daily living (ADLs) or instrumental activities of daily living (IADLs), or specified functional activities;
3 One or more selected impairments; or
4 Limitation in the ability to work around the house or at a job or business.

The overall findings of the study are as follows:

Among males aged 18–44 years, 10.3% reported some type of disability.
Among females aged 18–44 years, 11.7% reported some type of disability.
Among males aged 45–65 years, 21. 8% reported some type of disability.
Among females aged 45–65 years, 25.9% reported some type of disability.
Among males aged >65 years, 45.3% reported some type of disability.
Among females aged >65 years, 56.5% reported some type of disability.[14]

Awareness of disabilities greatly improved since the enactment of the Americans with Disabilities Act of 1990. The act introduced accommodation and accessibility standards, among many other benefits, for public and private establishments in order to help individuals with disabilities continue with their contributions to work and society in general. Among the most important aspects of the Americans with Disabilities Act of 1990 is raising awareness about the contributions of people with disabilities.[15]

Common Stereotypes

- Disabled individuals do not perform as well as others without disabilities.
- Disabled individuals are difficult to train properly.
- Disabled individuals are evaluated with lower standards than abled individuals.
- Disabled individuals are rewarded differently than abled individuals.
- Disabled individuals are treated differently than abled individuals.

Inclusion Tips and Resources

- Become informed about disabilities.
- Welcome disabled individuals into your groups and teams.
- Avoid perpetuating the stereotypes about disabled individuals.
- Organizations that have information:
  - www.usa.gov (List of Federal Agencies)

Sexual Orientation—Gay, Lesbian, Bisexual and Transgender

Who Are They?

The U.S. Equal Employment Opportunity commission is in charge of supporting laws that provide

equal opportunity in federal employment for all persons, to prohibit discrimination in employment because of race, color, religion, sex, national origin, handicap, age, sexual orientation or status as a parent, and to promote the full realization of equal employment opportunity through a continuing affirmative program in each executive department and agency. This policy of equal opportunity applies to and must be an integral part of every aspect of personnel policy and practice in the employment, development, advancement, and treatment of civilian employees of the federal government, to the extent permitted by law.[16]

Although this policy legally applies only to employees of the federal government, many businesses and other organizations have adopted portions of this statement in their codes of ethics and company policies.

Regardless of the legal and ethical implications, discrimination in the work environment due to the sexual orientation of an individual can negatively impact productivity in group and team work.[17] The term sexual orientation includes gay, lesbian, bisexual and transgender (GLBT). Gay is the word used to refer to both men and women who are sexually attracted to others of the same sex. The word *lesbian* specifically refers to women who are sexually attracted to other women. Joe Kort, a psychotherapist and professor of gay and lesbian studies at Wayne State University, writes the following:

> Appropriate terminology to use with gay clients no longer includes sexual preference or alternative lifestyle. Preference implies that it is a choice—which it is not—and heterosexuality is the alternative lifestyle for gays and lesbians. The correct word is sexual and romantic orientation. Homosexual is as offensive as would be the words negro and colored would be to an African-American today or crippled once was used to describe physically challenged individuals and would be offensive if used today. The correct word is gay and lesbian.[18]

Bisexual refers to individuals who are attracted to both men and women. *Transgender* is a term used to describe individuals who do not identify with conventional descriptions of male or female genders.

It is estimated that two thirds of GLBT employees in the workforce do not reveal their "true identity" because they fear antigay violence, alienation and being passed over for promotions. The fear, anxiety and tension caused by antigay sentiments in the workplace inevitably leads to losses in productivity and employee morale. Although the fight to protect homosexuals in the workplace continues in the courts, the fact remains that the majority of the population in the United States is heterosexual. Laws do not tend to change how people feel about people who are different than the majority. The advocates for equality in the workplace continue to stress the importance of job performance instead of sexual orientation.[19]

Common Stereotypes

- GLBT individuals are psychologically unstable.
- GLBT individuals are sexually promiscuous.
- GLBT individuals are sexual predators.
- GLBT individuals are not interested in long-term relationships.[20]

Inclusion Tips and Resources

- Seek out reliable information about GLBT individuals.
- Include GLBT individuals in groups and teams.
- Avoid perpetuating GLBT stereotypes by speaking up.
- Organizations that have information:
  - http://www.glaad.org/ (Gay and Lesbian Alliance Against Defamation)
  - http://www.pflag.org/ (Parents, Families and Friends of Lesbians and Gays)
  - www.usa.gov (List of Federal Agencies)
  - www.**gender**advocates.org/links/state_local.html

Military Experience—Spent Time in the Military Service

Who Are They?

U.S. Army
- The Army is the nation's principle land force.
- Provides combat operations on land in all environments and types of terrain, including complex urban environments, in order to defeat enemy ground forces, and seize, occupy and defend land areas.
- Operates within more than 120 countries to date.
- Current Responsibilities include:
  - Securing the South Korea border.
  - Keeping peace in Kosovo.
  - Defeating adversaries in Iraq and Afghanistan.
- Personnel:
  - 488,000 active duty soldiers deployed world-wide.
  - 189,000 Army reserves.
  - 346,000 Army National Guard.
- Slogan: "Army Strong."

U.S. Navy
- The Navy fights on the water, under the water and over the water.
- Every day, tens of thousands of Sailors and Marines and about 40 percent of all Navy ships are far from home.

- Current responsibilities include:
  - Protecting allies from ballistic missile attack in the Pacific, Arabian Gulf and the Mediterranean.
  - Catching drug smugglers in the Caribbean.
  - Building new partnerships in South America, Southeast Asia and Africa.
  - Flying our Navy planes, launched from carriers sailing the Indian Ocean, for about one-third of the close-air support missions that protect our Soldiers and Marines on the ground in Afghanistan.
- Personnel:
  - 330,000 active duty.
  - 120,000 Reservists deployed.
- Slogan: "A global force for good".

U.S. Marine Corps
- The Marine Corps is responsible for providing power projection from the sea, utilizing the mobility of the U.S. Navy to rapidly deliver combined-arms task forces to global crises.
- A part of the Navy Department, the Marines are the smallest of the United States Armed Forces in the Department of Defense.
- Current responsibilities include:
  - Serving as sea-based, integrated air-ground units for contingency and combat operations.
  - Flying fighter jets based on Navy amphibious ships, nicknamed "big decks," as well as drive tanks and ground vehicles.
- Personnel:
  - 190,000 active duty Marines.
  - 40,000 Marine Corps Reservists.
- Slogan: "The Few, The Proud".

U.S. Air Force
- The Air Force mission is to fly, fight and win . . . in air, space and cyberspace.
- The Air Force is the newest service, formed just 64 years ago in 1947 when the Army Air Corps became an independent Air Force.
- The Air Force has 3 core competencies—developing Airmen, technology-to-warfighting, integrating operations.
- Current responsibilities include:
  - Protecting American airspace after September 11.

- Supporting air and ground combat ops since 2001 for Operation Enduring Freedom and Operation Iraqi Freedom.
- Personnel:
  - 324,000 active duty.
  - 177,000 Air National Guard and Reservists.
- Slogan: "Aim High. Fly, Fight, Win".

U.S. Coast Guard

- The Coast Guard is a military, multi-mission, maritime service with maritime safety and security operations, marine environmental protection, waterways management, and regulatory functions as well as homeland security and national defense operations.
- The Coast Guard provides direct support to the Department of Defense and functions as a specialized service in the Department of the Navy in a time of declared war or by executive order.
- Current responsibilities include:
  - Port waterways and coastal security.
  - Drug and migrant interdiction.
  - Aids to navigation.
  - Performing search and rescue operations and marine environmental protection.
  - Providing defense readiness and law enforcement operations.
  - Located within the Department of Homeland Security, the Coast Guard is the only military service with statutory authority to enforce domestic U.S. laws.
- Personnel:
  - 42,390 active-duty members.
  - 6,945 reservists.
- Slogan: "Born Ready".

U.S. National Guard

- The Army and Air Force National Guard, organized by state, are the first military responders for domestic crises like Hurricane Katrina.
- The Guard provides 35–40 percent of the Army and Air Force operational forces, serving in locations like Afghanistan and Iraq.
- Current responsibilities include:
  - Providing wartime military support.

- Performing humanitarian, peacekeeping, and homeland security missions.
- Members of the National Guard, as well as the Reserves, return to their civilian jobs in between activation periods.
- Personnel:
  - 460,000 Soldiers and Airmen, located in over 3,300 American communities.
- Slogan: "Always ready. Always there."

In addition to the active members of the military:

- There are 1.9 million children, ranging in ages from newborn to 18 years old, who are the children of our military—1.3 million of whom are school aged.
- Of our military children, 765,000 have active-duty parents and 225,000 with a parent who is currently deployed.
- 73,000 service members are active-duty single parents, and 40,000 are active-duty dual-military parents.
- Military spouses face enormous employment challenges as they relocate due to assignments of duty locations. Spouses often are not able to maintain their own careers due to relocations since they face the immediate need to maintain their households. This means finding a job instead of following a career.

List of military services and families of the military.[21]

Common Stereotypes

- People in the military are usually rigid and think that there is only one way to complete assignments.
- Those in the military only know how to give and take orders. They do not know how to think.
- Individuals with military experience do not have business savvy.
- In the military, individuals are spoiled by having unlimited resources.
- The senior members of the military behave like prima donnas.[22]

Inclusion Resources

- Organizations that have information:
  - www.va.gov/opa/militaryfamilies.asp (Department of Veterans Affairs)
  - www.dol.gov/vets/ (Department of Labor, Veterans' Employment and Training Services)

- www.samhsa.gov/militaryfamilies/ (Substance Abuse and Mental Health Services Administration)
- www.sba.gov/veterans-and-military-families (Small Business Administration Veterans and Military Families)
- www.state.gov/militaryfamilies/index.htm (Helping Military Families and Veterans: Programs at the U.S. Department of State)
- www.usa.gov/ (List of Federal Agencies)

Personality—Set of Individual Characteristics

Who Are They?

The world of work is so diverse, that even an individual's personality is now considered a dimension of diversity. Personality is generally defined as the set of characteristics included in patterns of behavior used to respond to ideas, objects, or people in our daily environment. The result of years of research fits the findings about personality into the Big Five personality factors described in Chapter 2 (extroversion, agreeableness, conscientiousness, emotional stability and openness to experience). One additional trait that is included recently in the score of personality research is likability. Likeability is a subset of the agreeableness trait that includes friendliness, cooperation, understanding of others and helping others with positive self-worth.[23]

Personality plays several important roles in how individuals work with others in groups and teams. Attitudes and behaviors are among the most important work-related attributes influenced by an individual's personality.

Attitudes and behaviors vary in individuals due to internal and external factors. Locus of control is one factor that determines how individual view their successes and failures. Individuals with an internal locus of control tend to place responsibility within themselves, and believe that they are in control of their destiny; one events at a time. On the other hand, those with an external locus of control tend to place responsibility on chance, luck, events or others.

Locus of control influences behavior in terms of productivity, leadership and team participation. Typically, internal locus of control type of individuals are motivated, can handle complex tasks such as problem solving and are more oriented toward success. Internal locus of control group members or team members also tend to be more independent and are less likely to value teamwork. People with an external locus of control tend to behave in opposite ways than internal locus of control individuals.

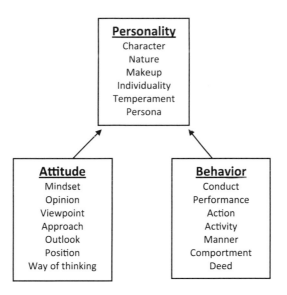

Figure 3.2

The purpose of describing personality, attitudes and behaviors is to provide some general information as it relates to working with diverse groups of people in achieving a common goal. The intricate details of studying behavior are better left to the experts. Yet, it is important to have some understanding of what makes people "tick." Consultant Deborah Hildebrand offers the following tips for working among people who will undoubtedly show up to work with their own version of a personality:

1   Understand your own personality and how you react to others.
2   Treat everyone with respect.
3   When leading a team or group, make sure everyone has an equal chance to participate.
4   Remember that everyone wants to fit in.[24]

Common Stereotypes

- Birth order and family size influence personality.
- Personality is stable throughout life.
- Personality is linked to certain illnesses.
- There are only five core personality traits.
- Personality is influenced by personal preferences.
- Facebook profiles are accurate descriptions of personalities.
- Pets reveal their master's personalities.[25]

Inclusion Resources

- Organizations that have information:
  - www.usa.gov (List of Federal Agencies)
  - www.apa.org (American Psychological Association)
  - www.spsp.org (Society for Personality and Social Psychology)

Diversity Exercise: Below is a list that describes individuals who have broken the various diversity components described in this chapter. Find the name of the individual that best matches the description. The names are listed below the chart. The correct answers are listed at the end of the chapter.

Table 3.5

Description	Name of Individual
First African American to head a Fortune 500 Company	
First Hispanic U.S. Supreme Court Justice	
Youngest elected U.S. President	
Oldest elected U.S. President	
Germany's first female leader	
Percentage of male registered nurses in the U.S.	
1993–2011	
News anchor, political commentator, TV host, PhD and first openly gay American to receive a Rhodes Scholarship	
World-famous blind pianist and singer	
Best female athlete with a disability	
First African American female combat pilot	
Went from being a Marine to chairman and CEO of FedEx	
Mathematician/physicist with a learning disability	
American journalist who suffers from clinical depression	

List of Names for the Exercise[26]

Franklin D. Raines	Sonia Sotomayor	John F. Kennedy
Ronald Reagan	Angela Merkel	Six
Stevie Wonder	Erin Popovich	Span of gays in the U.S. Military, "Don't Ask, Don't Tell"

Rachel Maddow   Vernice Armour   Frederick W. Smith
Albert Einstein   Mike Wallace

Chapter 3 introduces elements of the diverse world in which we live and work. The information is intended to introduce group and team members to the complexity of working with others toward a common goal. Three suggestions for improvement in this area include:

- Avoid making assumptions about others: Do not assume that others will act the same way you act.
- Avoid making judgments: When others act differently than what you are used to, do not automatically think they are wrong.
- Honor differences: Learn about other cultures and practices to determine the best possible course of action.[27]

Review Questions

1   Describe seven types of stereotypes found in today's work environment.
2   Why is it important to learn about diversity in the workplace?
3   Regarding each type of stereotype described in Chapter 3, select one of the suggested resources and research the resource online. What new information did you find?
4   Explain the relationship between personality and diversity in the workplace.

Note: Answers to the Review Questions and Diversity Exercise are located in the Appendix.

Chapter 4 will further expand the dynamics of team building by adding yet another layer to the elements of the individual and diverse group or team members: team building.

Notes

*   History Channel. (1977). Jimmy Carter on human rights [Audio clip]. Retrieved from http://www.history.com/speeches/jimmy-carter-on-human-rights#jimmy-carter-on-human-rights

1. Marqius, J. (2008, February 27). Companies opt for surface diversity. *HRM Guide US Human Resources.* Retrieved from http://www.hrmguide.com/diversity/surface-diversity.htm

2. Bell, S.T., Villado, A.J., Lukasik, M.A., Belau, L. & Briggs, A. L. (2011). Getting specific about demographic diversity variable and team performance relationships: A meta-analysis. *Journal of Management, 37,* 709. Retrieved from jom.sagepub.com

3. Thompson, L.L. (2004). Making the team (2nd ed.). Upper Saddle River, NJ: Pearson Education.

4. Daft, R. (2010). *Management* (10th ed.) Mason, OH: South-Western.

5. Center for Immigration Studies. (2007, November 8). *Immigrants in the United States, 2007: A profile of America's foreign born population.* Retrieved from http://www.cis.org/immigration

6. U.S. Department of State. *Types of visas for temporary visitors.* (2003, May 1). Retrieved from http://travel.state.gov/visa/temp/types/types_1286.html

7. Szu-Hsien, C., & Klemer, B. H. (2003). Common racial stereotypes. *Equal Opportunities International, 22*(3).

8. U.S. Department of Commerce, Economics and Statistics Administration, U.S. Census Bureau. (2011, May). Age and sex composition. Retrieved from http://www.census.gov/pr

9. Tolbize, A. (2008). *Generational differences in the workplace.* Minneapolis, MN: Research and Training Center, University of Minnesota. Retrieved from http://rtc.umn.edu/docs/2_18_Gen_diff_workplace.pdf

10. Posthuma, R.A., & Campion, M.A. (2009). Age stereotypes in the workplace: Common stereotypes, moderators, and future research directions? *Journal of Management, 35,* 158. Retrieved from http://jom.sagepub.com.libweb.lib.utsa.edu/content/35/1/158.full.pdf+html

11. U.S. Department of Commerce et al.

12. *Gender differences.* (2004). Retrieved from http://www.enotes.com/topic/Gender_differences

13. *Gender differences.*

14. Center for Disease Control and Prevention. (2005). *Prevalence and most common causes of disability among adults, United States.* Retrieved from http://www.cdc.gov/mmwr/preview/mmwrhtml/mm5816a2.htm

15. U.S. Department of Justice. (1990, July 26). *Americans with Disabilities Act.* Retrieved from http://www.ada.gov/index.html

16. U.S. Equal Employment Opportunity Commission. (2001). *Facts about discrimination based on sexual orientation, status as a parent, marital status and political affiliation.* Retrieved from www.eeoc.gov/federal/otherprotections.cfm

17. Kort, Joe. (2008). Alienation or affirmation: 10 common mistakes straight clinicians make when working with gays and lesbians. *Psychology Today.* Retrieved from http://www.psychologytoday.com/

18. Bauer, M., & Kleiner, B.H. (2001). New developments concerning sexual orientation issues in the workplace. *Opportunities International, 20,* 5–7.

19. Felmlee, D., Orzechowicz, D., & Fortes, C. (2010). Fairy tales: Attraction and stereotypes in same-gender relationships. *Sex Roles, 62*, 226–240.
20. OURMILITARY.MIL: Connecting You With Your Military. (n.d.). *Our services* [Web site]. Retrieved from http://www.ourmilitary.mil/learn/our-services/
21. Safani, B. (2011). Five common military stereotypes debunked. *Military Families Week.* Retrieved from http://jobs.aol.com/articles/2011/04/15/five-common-military- stereotypes-debunked/
22. Daft, R. 10th ed.
23. Hildebrand, D. S. (2007). *Managing different personalities.* Retrieved from http://www.suite101.com/content/managing-different-personalities a24620
24. Cherry, K. (n.d.). *10 fascinating facts about personality.* About.com: Psychology [Web site]. Retrieved from http://psychology.about.com/od/personalitydevelopment/tp/facs-about-personality.htm
25. Bovee, C. L., & Thill, J. V. (2012). *Business communication today.* Boston, MA: Pearson.
26. Examples of individuals for the Diversity Exercise where retrieved from www.answers.yahoo.com/search.

4

Team Competency

What You Need to Know About the Team Environment

If you want to build a ship, don't drum up people together to collect wood and don't assign them tasks and work, but rather teach them to long for the endless immensity of the sea.

—**Antoine de Saint-Exupery***

Introduction

Chapter 4 introduces the fourth building block for developing effective teams. Remember the insights you gained in previous chapters, as these will help sustain your progress as you move on to new information.

Human beings have worked in groups and teams for as long as recorded history can validate. Primitive tribes counted on teamwork for survival just as factories during the industrial age used work groups and teams to improve efficiencies in productivity.[1] In today's environment, working with others includes a variety of technological advances that have made the experience both rewarding and challenging. Working with others to achieve a common goal can be frustrating at the very least. Yet, research studies originating in the 1950s continue to support the benefits of teamwork on many levels.[2] The quote at the beginning of the chapter emphasizes the importance of developing the interpersonal skills within a group or team to focus on a common goal.

While the individual's technical and subject matter skills are equally important, this chapter will address the human skills.

Chapter 4 Competencies

The purpose of this chapter is to help you:
- Know the difference between groups and teams.
- Understand the 10 key challenges faced by group and team members.
- Describe the five steps of team development.
- Learn how to manage five team dysfunctions.

Figure 4.1

Groups and Teams

The most important aspect of groups and teams is that they all come together to accomplish a common goal. The primary difference between groups and teams lies in the process of how the work is managed to achieve a common goal. Groups are usually much more structured than teams. For example, groups tend to follow the structure of the organization that they represent. Groups tend to have designated roles, individual accountability and individual work products. Teams usually do not adhere to traditional organizational structures. Team members often collaborate on products by sharing both the work and the accountability for a job well done.[3]

Whether work is completed by a group or a team, there are certain sets of knowledge, skills and abilities or competencies that serve to assure effectiveness and efficiency in both environments. The following exercise serves to help individuals reflect on past experiences in working with groups and teams.

Exercise: Group and Team Experience

Use the Chart to Respond to the Following

1 List a team or group in which you participate or have participated under the first column (Team/Group Identification).
2 Circle the best answer for each group or team from the two choices provided in the second and third columns.
3 Review the answers to determine the effectiveness of the group or team.
4 Repeat by adding another team or group name in the first column.

Chart for Exercise: Group and Team Experience

Table 4.1

Team/Group Identification	Effectiveness Characteristic	Noneffectiveness Characteristic
	Communication	No communication
	Trust	No trust
	Conflict managed	Conflict out of control
	Commitment	No commitment
	Accountability	No accountability
	Results focused	Nobody cares
	Time management	No time management
	High morale	Low morale
	Common goals	No goals
	Respect	Lack of respect

Exercise Reflection: The effectiveness of your group/team experience depends on how many items were identified from the column labeled "effectiveness characteristics." All groups and teams face challenges at one time or another. If choices exist, conflict will usually follow. The key to effective group/team work is to increase effectiveness by managing the noneffective characteristics. Ignoring issues only worsens the situation.

Tips and Resources for Managing "Noneffective Characteristics" or Challenges of Groups and Teams

No Communication

Chapter 5 is dedicated to the topic of communication; yet, a few comments are also included in Chapter 4 due to the role that communication plays in developing effective groups and teams. Communication skills are at the core of everything we do, individually and in our interactions with others.

Business communication is of utmost importance because the failure to communicate effectively can lead to significant consequences. Jobs are jeopardized, time is wasted, money is lost and relationships are adversely impacted when business communication fails to achieve a purpose. More detailed information is found in Chapter 5.

Tips for Improving Business Communication

- Give your audience information they can use.
- Be clear and accurate with information. Stick to the facts and avoid opinions. Emotions have no place in business communication.
- Keep your messages concise.
- Let your audience know what you expect from them and what they can expect from you.
- Clearly describe how the parties involved in the communication will benefit from positive results.[4]

No Trust

Much is said about trust, but what does it truly mean? To trust usually falls into a continuum. Think about those in whom you place your trust. Where would you place them on the following scale?

Minimum Trust————Some Trust————More Trust————Implicit Trust

Consider the following questions:

1   Minimum Trust

    a   Why did you select this category?
    b   What happened to cause you to minimally trust someone?
    c   What will it take to move this person to another point on the scale?

2   Some Trust

    a   Why did you select this category?
    b   What happened to cause you to have some trust in someone?
    c   What will it take to move this person to another point on the scale?

3   More Trust

    a   Why did you select this category?
    b   What happened to cause you to have more trust someone?
    c   What will it take to move this person to another point on the scale?

4   Implicit Trust

    a   Why did you select this category?
    b   What happened to cause you to trust someone implicitly?
    c   What will it take to keep this person at this level on the scale?

Trust is based on many and varied characteristics; both personal and environmental characteristics and circumstances. Studies indicate that "The most fundamental determinants of trust however, are openness, honesty consistency, and respect."[5] The most difficult aspect of trust development is that it is a give and take proposition. Someone has to take the first step in developing trust, and that is likely the most difficult step. An individual must be prepared to share information openly, reveal feelings and take a risk. Building trust is an individual choice.

Conflict Out of Control

Conflict is to be expected in building relationships with others, and building relationships is the cornerstone of teamwork. A misconception about conflict is that it can be resolved. Therefore, the goal in addressing conflict is to think in terms of managing not resolving the conflict.

Research indicates that a certain amount of conflict is actually beneficial in terms of creativity and productivity. Therefore, the issue is not the conflict itself. The issue is how individuals behave during a conflict. A conflict that results in cooperation and increased productivity is called positive or constructive conflict. The opposite is negative or destructive behavior which usually leads to lack of respect, decreases in productivity and even bullying.[6] Positive and negative behaviors in conflict management depend on an individual's personality, past experiences and a number of other traits and characteristics. One way to determine behavioral reactions to conflict is through self-assessments.

Numerous studies validate the importance of learning about behavioral characteristics. The more we know about ourselves and others improves how we manage situations, such as conflict. The *Thomas-Kilmann Conflict Mode Instrument* (TKI) is one of the most widely used self-assessments that provides feedback on conflict behaviors. Most instruments, on the other hand, assess conflict management styles. The key to understanding conflict management is to begin by understanding the behavioral reactions that individuals exhibit when faced with a conflict. The TKI, which has been in the market for more than 30 years, is based on two primary dimensions of behavior, assertiveness and cooperativeness. Once the assessment is completed, the analysis offers five possible ways in which to respond to conflict: competing, accommodating, avoiding, collaborating and compromising. Taking this assessment adds value to an individual's approach toward understanding and managing conflict in any situation. The results of the TKI approach conflict management as an event that can be addressed with any of the five approaches, depending on the individual's personality, the environment and the shared goals of those in conflict.[7] For more information about the TKI, visit the author's Web site at http://www. kilmanndiagnostics.com/catalog/thomas-kilmann-conflict-mode-instrument.

Tips for effective conflict management:

- Communication: Listen first—talk later. Individuals who disagree tend to be easy to anger. When you listen to the other person's side first, it is likely that the other party will be more willing to listen to your side.
- Common goals: Find a common goal to serve as the purpose for managing the conflict. Regardless of each party's position or feelings about the conflict, focusing on a common goal or common ground serves to establish a positive outcome.
- Control your fear: Everybody wants to be right, and everyone wants to be liked. Put aside the fear of the unknown because disclosure will help you identify a common goal.
- Positive intent: A positive attitude about your intentions and the intentions of others establishes a platform for best results in managing conflicts.

- Win–win mind set: Strive to reach a win–win approach to the conflict. Concentrate on common ground and common goals as these provide the foundation for positive conflict management.[8]

No Commitment

Commitment is another foundation for effective team work. A commitment can be anything from a legally binding contract to a personal promise or handshake. When an individual commits to something, it means that energy, knowledge, skill and ability are dedicated to a successful outcome.

Exercise: Define commitment by listing as many examples of words that are associated with the word (synonyms). In addition list words that are the opposite of commitment (antonyms).

Table 4.2

Commitment	Synonyms	Antonyms
Assure	Promise	Deny
Intention	Obligation	Indifference
Promise	Give your word	Lie

Use the commitment words listed above to describe groups and teams in past experiences. The productive and successful experiences will include many of the synonyms in the first column. The unproductive and unsuccessful experiences will include many of the antonyms from the second column. Use these words as a checklist when preparing to engage in group or team activity to increase the chances for success. Commitment is another personal choice, and individual contributions are what make a group or team experience meaningful.

No Accountability

Businesses around the world use the term accountability for strategy and planning to insure that business employees, processes and products are designed and managed to achieve a return on investment for the organization. In the context of working well with others, accountability has the same meaning. Accountability is the measurement of the contributions of each participant in achieving common goals.

Accountability is associated with fairness, honesty and responsibility, both to oneself and to others. When individuals are accountable, they do what they say they are going to do. This promise of accountability can be supported by establishing performance management principles such as those found in organizations where productivity is measured against strategic, tactical, functional and individual goals. However, the path that leads to fulfillment of higher level goals depends on the input of individuals. In a group or team, individuals can provide valuable knowledge, skills and abilities, one person at a time.

Tips for Individual Accountability

- Approach group or team work as a partnership where every individual is an equal contributor and achiever.
- Socialization is important; be deliberate about getting to know each other.
- Select group and team members who have similar interests in doing a good job.
- Select group and team members who have the knowledge, skills and abilities needed for the job.
- Celebrate accomplishments frequently to maintain morale and motivation.
- Make sure that tasks are equitably shared by everyone.
- Share strengths by coaching each other.[9]

Lack of Focus—Nobody Cares

In a work environment, to care means to show concern and empathy for others. It does not mean that you have to take them home; just find a way to focus on the group's objective.

Fuqua and Newman,[10] psychology researchers and consultants, suggest that successful organizations are comprised of systems in which employees can excel when certain practices prevail. The practices include the following:

- Gratitude—When people who work together are grateful, they focus on positive elements of the circumstances that surround them. This, in turn, creates a broader perspective with which to deal with challenging situations.
- Forgiveness—Simply stated, the failure to forgive leads to anger and conflict. Therefore, forgiving others can be viewed as a practical matter. Working with others can lead to unintentional infringements, and the expectation of forgiveness can add valuable energy to interactions that help improve morale and productivity.

- Encouragement—Encouragement is everyone's responsibility, not just a management responsibility. From a practical standpoint, peer encouragement is more abundant and available due to the working environment. This is a rich source of motivation for and by team and group members.
- Compassion—When individuals share supportive behaviors, tension is reduced and a form of camaraderie develops to support the working environment.
- Community—Maintain a balance between individual motivations and group/team goals. Both individual and group/team goal achievement increases as the two become more aligned.
- Tolerance—Avoid having expectations that are rigid and unreasonable. Everybody is different; with varying needs, wants and backgrounds.
- Inclusion—Including everyone in idea generation, planning, strategizing, productivity and celebrations reduces stress. When everyone is busy because they feel included, there is little time to be negative.
- Charity—Giving to group and team members does not have to consist of material things. Sometimes the best gifts are time, patience, recognition and friendliness. Be kind; it's free and goes a long way.

Exercise: Reflection helps establish positive thoughts and provides a plan for positive intentions. Use the chart below to reflect on those characteristics that are easy to practice. Also, follow up with a plan to address those characteristics that are more difficult to practice.

These characteristics are easy to practice:

Table 4.3

Caring Characteristic	Example	Result
Gratitude	I am thankful for my job because of the challenges I face each day.	I am curious about what will happen each day.
Forgiveness		
Encouragement		
Compassion		
Community		
Tolerance		
Inclusion		
Charity		

These characteristics are difficult to practice:

Table 4.4

Caring Characteristic	Example	Result
Gratitude	I hate going to work!	I do not look forward to going to work each day.
Forgiveness		
Encouragement		
Compassion		
Community		
Tolerance		
Inclusion		
Charity		

Review the results of each exercise and think about ways to continue doing what is working well. Also, think about the unfavorable results from the exercise. Think about ways to improve or change the conditions for a more favorable outcome.

No Time Management

Time management is about using time wisely; this is a choice. Good planning can improve choices, assuming there are no extenuating circumstances. Nevertheless, planning is a good habit to practice because it reduces wasting energy on unproductive activities. One aspect of time that is often overlooked is that there are only 24 hours in a day, and absolutely nothing can add even a second to that day.

Exercise: How Do You Spend Time During a Given Day?

Step 1: Read the following list of typical activities and estimate the amount of time spent on each activity.

Step 2: Proceed to the chart provided. Each block in the chart represents one hour of time, and the whole chart represents a twenty-four hour day. Review the list of activities from Step 1 and shade in the amount of time consumed by each activity.

Step 1: List of Typical Daily Activities:

1   Personal (grooming, eating, going to the restroom, meals, etc.) _____ hours/minutes

2   Travel (driving, commuting, traffic, etc.) _____ hours/minutes

3   Work outside the home _____ hours/minutes
4   Work inside the home _____ hours/minutes
5   School and studying _____ hours/minutes
6   Socializing _____ hours/minutes
7   Entertainment (theater, movies, social media, etc.) _____ hours/minutes
8   Shopping _____ hours/minutes
9   Sleeping _____ hours/minutes
10   Other _____ hours/minutes
     Total hours/minutes _____

Step 2: Each block in the following chart represents one hour of time, and the chart represents a 24-hour day. Shade in the amount of time spent in each of the activities listed above.

Many people who complete this exercise run out of time before getting to the end of the listed activities. Having more to do than time allows seems to be a guaranteed part of everyday life. The current mantra is to "do more with less." Regardless of the technological advances used to maximize productivity, the current state of affairs regarding time leaves most individuals exhausted, frustrated and stressed. All of these conditions are seriously detrimental to productivity, but most of all to an individual's health.

Time-management skills are fundamental in the fight against time. Learn and practice time-management skills that will serve in so many ways to alleviate stress related conditions. As a result other positive consequences will include improvements in work habits and productivity. Overall, the most important benefit is that time-management skills improve the quality of life for those who learn and practice the skills.

Tips for Effective Time Management

- Research and read about time management.
- Learn what the experts are doing; what works and what does not work.
- Talk to your family and group/team members about your time-management concerns.

- Assess how you spend your time on a day-to-day basis.
- Make a record of your daily tasks so that you can see what you have created.
- Make tough decisions about what is really important.
- Ask for help; don't try to do it all yourself.
- Practice saying *no*; this is part of learning to ask for help.
- Be creative about how you proceed through your daily tasking.
- Regarding paperwork, do not pick up a piece of paper unless you intend to do something with it.
- Practice, even if you have to start over at the beginning every day.

Low Morale

A survey conducted by a management professor from Wichita State University revealed five characteristics in the work environment that support high morale. The five characteristics include:

1 Personal appreciation from a manager.
2 Written appreciation from a manager.
3 Performance-based promotions.
4 Public acknowledgement.
5 Meetings that build morale.[11]

Clearly, these are characteristics that apply to working in a group or team. These characteristics take into consideration the knowledge, skills and abilities that have been described so far in this and previous chapters. Basic interpersonal skills and practices are at the root of each characteristic.

Each group or team member brings his or her own set of perspectives to work, and high or low morale is one of the ingredients. Morale is not something that you can physically or emotionally give to each member of your group/team. Yet, it is possible to create an environment where morale is uplifted, practiced and maintained.

In addition to adhering to work-related practices and policies, research shows that one of the most effective ways to raise and maintain high morale is with appropriate use of humor. Funny things happen every day; it is a matter of being open to having a humor perspective. Dr. Michael Purinton, Dean of Education, St. Johns River Community College, offers seven suggestions for developing a humor perspective:

1 Share your humanity with others by talking about personal funny experiences.

2   Include humorous quotations in your discussions, meetings and other activities.
3   Collect and post funny cartoons that are appropriate and relevant to your work environment.
4   Create and share humorous "Top 10 Lists" that suit your environment.
5   Collect and share funny mistakes from newspapers and other sources to lighten up meetings or gatherings.
6   Save and share entertaining memos, letters and cards.
7   Think of funny ways to say potentially negative comments.[12]

Tips for Maintaining a High-Morale Work Environment

- Make sure that each participant feels valued.
- Set and follow policies and procedures.
- Set achievable and realistic goals.
- Talk about individual contributions.
- Discuss accountability and consequences.
- Help each other; collaborate.
- Praise accomplishments of all types.
- Celebrate small and large milestone accomplishments.
- Practice appropriate humor. Having fun and being productive are not mutually exclusive.
- Communicate, communicate, communicate.

No Goals

Goals are the stepping stones that lead groups/teams to success. Goals help set expectations, and expectations help identify the individual contributions necessary for accomplishing a common goal. Setting realistic and achievable goals is a skill that can be learned and practiced with frequent use. Basically, goals should be specific and measurable. They should clearly state what needs to be done, the time allowed for completion of the tasks and a way to determine (measure) the results. The difficulty of a goal should be somewhere between too easy and too difficult; in other words, challenging. It is also very important that everyone in the work group participates in goal setting. This increases inclusion and accountability. Also, be sure to include a progress monitoring component in goals. Assess the progress made in achieving goals by providing continuous and mutual feedback.[13]

Robbins and Hunsaker[14], in their book about providing tips for managing people at work, share seven steps for setting goals:

1 Be specific about what you need to accomplish by identifying the tasks that will lead your group to success. This step is similar to writing a job description for each group/team member.
2 Specifically define the measurements that will be used to assess performance on each task.
3 Describe the expectations of each group/team member regarding specific targets that each individual should reach.
4 Identify the deadlines for specific goal accomplishments; individually and as a group or team.
5 When there are several goals, determine the order in which they should be completed through ranking the goals by level of importance.
6 Determine the level of difficulty of each goal to insure equitability in assigning and assessing work.
7 When goal completion depends on input from outside entities, make sure to coordinate such efforts to avoid conflict and other delays.

Lack of Respect

Define respect:
Give an example of a time when you felt respected by others:

Give an example of a time when you felt disrespected by others:

Give an example of a time when you showed respect for someone:

Give an example of a time when you disrespected someone:

Thinking about respect is useful to determine an individual's perspective regarding respect. Doirean Wilson of Middlesex University Business School in the United Kingdom writes about a review of the literature in "What Price, Respect." She summarizes the definitions of respect to include behavior that is considerate of others' feelings. Implicit in these definitions are moral values and dignity.[15]

Working in groups and teams inevitably partners individual with others from different cultures, upbringings, religions and numerous other characteristics.

Treating others with respect can be as simple as using the same techniques and approaches that one would want from others. This is not always an easy task; yet, the alternative usually results in negativity, anger, dysfunction and loss of productivity.

In his business blog, Small Business Trends, Jack Yoest makes reference to respect as the "the ultimate business etiquette".[16] The trend that Yoest describes in 2006 has continued in its downward spiral since then. The lack of basic common courtesies, such as saying "thank you" and "please" is at an epidemic level. What happened to making eye contact with another human being instead of looking at the electronic gadget in your hand? Another lost art is paying attention, simply listening, when someone is speaking. Those who maintain a high regard for the simple tried and true common courtesies in the workplace and in society know the secret to the human condition: it does not change. As the world changes, human beings maintain their basic needs to be liked, to be right and to be heard.

Respect takes time and effort, on everyone's part. A fundamental concept like respect is difficult to develop because it is part of relationship building. One party has to begin the process, and the other party needs to reciprocate. It is worth the investment in time and effort in order to reap the self-respect benefits that in turn help fuel the ongoing effort.

To sum up this section, respect, in a nutshell, is a critical ingredient for success in working with others. It might be useful to see the process of creating and maintaining respect as a three step approach to interpersonal relationships as illustrated in the following diagram. The beginning of the process should start with oneself followed by including others. Nothing good will happen without sound communication skills, such as listening to and understanding others. The third step is about nurturing two of the most sought after and valued interpersonal characteristics: integrity and trust.

Steps Toward Building Respect

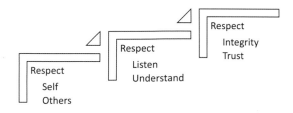

Figure 4.2

Types of Groups and Teams

There are two primary levels of groups that exist within organizations: formal groups and informal groups. Formal groups are those that are created and managed by management or by the organization to help achieve organizational goals and objectives. Informal groups usually develop due to individual efforts and friendships among people, and although they serve to promote organizational objectives, they are not deliberately created by the organization.

Formal groups are designed to follow the processes of the organization. These usually fall into one of two types: command groups and task groups. Command groups serve to describe the groupings of people set by the relationship between a manager or supervisor and the individuals who report to them. A task group exists to complete a specific task or project.

Informal groups come together based on similar interests and when friendships develop among coworkers. Both interest and friendship groups help individuals with a basic need to socialize with one another. At the same time, these informal groups can be useful in adding support to the formal groups of an organization.[17] The existence and value of groups has been studied widely over the years. Researchers are mostly interested in why groups form and whether they add value to organizational goals. Like other aspects of human beings and organizations, it all depends on a number of variables. In general, people tend to join groups for interpersonal interaction, to participate in group goals and for economic reasons, such a group work incentives.[18]

A variety of types of teams exist in a typical work environment. The most common types of teams include problem-solving teams, cross-functional teams, virtual teams and self-managed teams. Regardless of the type of team, all of them have a few things in common. Teams consist of members who have a common goal and who share complementary sets of knowledge, skills and abilities in their efforts to complete goals.

Problem-solving teams are usually temporary and are formed to focus on a particular problem. Once the problem is addressed, the cross-functional team members return to their typical duties. Cross-functional teams are formed by assigning individuals from different departments to work together on a project that affects a number of areas within the organization. These teams last longer than problem-solving teams. The common practice calls for rotating team members in and out of a cross-functional team if the tasks continue for extended periods of time.

Virtual teams are composed of team members who are geographically separated and use technology to communicate. The purpose of virtual teams is to improve efficiency and task effectiveness for the organization. Self-managed teams are formed when the organization's culture supports the type of work that is self-directed. It does not mean that teams have no leadership or management. Self-managed team members must have knowledge, skill and ability sets that are mature in that their responsibilities include self-management in addition to task completion.[19]

Stages of Development

Groups and teams tend to experience similar stages of development. Studies continually analyze team development progress, and one of the most popular models is summarized in a five stage development process.[20] The five stages include:

Table 4.5

Development Stage	Description
Forming	Group and team members get to know each other.
Storming	Group and team members begin to discuss, argue and position themselves.
Norming	Group and team members establish expectations and consequences for behavior.
Performing	Group and team members reach maturity and focus on productivity.
Adjourning	Group and team members finish their task and end their association.

The five-stage model can serve as a guideline for new groups and teams. Since no two groups or teams are the same, the actual progress of development can differ. Research has yet to conclusively identify clear parameters of team development such as the length of time each of the stages take or should take. These guidelines are useful in helping groups and teams understand that certain developmental stages will and should occur.

Group and Team Dysfunctions

Just as teams tend to follow clear stages of development, they also experience common dysfunctions. Some of the most frequent occurrences are briefly described in the following section. The dysfunctions include groupthink, free riders, conflict, meetings and difficult people.

Groupthink—Groupthink occurs when a group or team develops an unhealthy closeness or allegiance to each other. One example of groupthink is when a group or team becomes so interested in supporting each other's ideas that they no longer consider different or challenging contributions to their progress.

Tips for Managing Groupthink

* Encourage and maintain open communication.
* Assign a team member the role of "gate keeper" to observe for signs of groupthink.
* Stay focused on team and organizational goals.

Free riders—Well-developed and organized groups and teams do not include free riders. Free riders do exist in some groups and teams, and they typically try to get credit for the work of the others without significant contributions.

Tips for Managing Free Riders

* Build accountability standards into the team goals and objectives.
* Conduct regular performance evaluations.
* Insist on open communication.
* Early on during team formation, make sure the team members have the set of skills, knowledge and abilities needed for team success.

Conflict—Conflict occurs when group or team members disagree. The different types of conflict and conflict management techniques will not resolve the potential for conflict. However, when individuals have conflict management skills, they will be able to manage conflict effectively to prevent losses in productivity and morale.

Tips for Managing Conflict

* Invest time during the initial meetings of your group or team in getting to know each other. The time you invest up front will make the group or team experience much more productive, pleasant and fun.
* Establish ground rules for team activities and interactions.

- Insist on open communication.
- Address issues early on; do not let issues lie dormant.

Meetings—Productive teamwork is often contingent upon meetings, and well-executed meetings are the key to maintaining progress among the team members. Unfortunately, meetings have a negative connotation due to the lack of preparation and execution. Organizations have a documented history of having too many meetings that waste valuable time and energy. The key to conducting effective meetings is to keep it simple. Determine the reason for meeting, make sure the right people are invited to attend, plan the content and format of the meeting, and be prepared to facilitate the meeting (manage time and document the proceedings).

Tips for Effective Meetings

- Determine the reason for meeting.
  - Why meet?
  - Does everyone involved know why the meeting is scheduled?
  - Is meeting the best way to address the situation?
  - Is the return on investment for the meeting going to add value?
- Make sure the right people are invited to attend.
  - How many people should attend?
  - Do attendees possess the right knowledge, skills and/or abilities?
- Plan the content and format of the meeting.
  - Create an agenda.
  - Develop and use a set of ground rules.
  - Distribute the agenda to the attendees before the meeting time.
  - Prepare those who will need to make contributions during the meeting.
  - Determine where the meeting will take place.
  - Acquire the necessary materials and equipment.
  - Identify a time keeper and a note taker.
  - Be prepared to facilitate the meeting.
  - Prepare an activity to help energize the participants (ice-breaker).
  - Determine and share the ground rules with attendees.[21]

Difficult People—Unfortunately, meetings and other interactions between team members can be challenging when people chose to be difficult. Dealing with difficult people is not a clear science.

Tips for Managing Difficult People

Table 4.6

Characteristic of Difficult People	Suggested Approach
Talkative, Domineering, Rambler	• Refer to the ground rules. • Say that time is running out. • Say that you must move on. • Privately talk to the individual about time issues. • Create smaller groups if possible. • Create an agenda of additional concerns for a future meeting.
Argumentative, Domineering, Questions everything	• Refer to ground rules. • Do not lose your composure. • Be patient, yet firm. • Provide time for discussions in the agenda. • Engage others in the discussion. • Privately talk with the individual about concerns.
Reserved, Quiet, Shy, Says nothing	• Refer to ground rules. • Be patient. • Ask the person a direct question. • Include opportunities to encourage participation. • Acknowledge participation.
Do-it-all, Let me do it, I will do it, I must do it all	• Refer to ground rules. • Encourage participation from others. • Be direct, and tell the person what would be a better group approach. • Discuss the issue openly with the rest of the group. • Talk to the person privately.
Free rider, Others will do it, Just along for the ride, Don't bother me with details	• Refer to ground rules. • Include activities to help engage everyone. • Talk privately with individual. • Discuss issues openly with all group members.
Personality clash, I just don't like you, You remind me of someone I don't like	• Refer to ground rules. • Maintain professionalism. • Talk with the individual privately. • Focus on the common goals of the group. • Discuss openly with whole group.

Chapter 4 provides basic information about working with others in a group or team environment. This basic approach serves to introduce the varied and complex aspects of working with others. Every efficient and effective group/team of individuals will go far if they build their relationships on solid basic skills. Chapter 5 introduces the benefits and challenges of effective communication. Communication is the "circulatory system" of teamwork in that positive and/or negative messages are quickly distributed throughout the members of a team. Effective communication analysis, tips for managing communication and the role of technology are discussed in Chapter 5.

Review Questions

1 Describe the main difference between groups and teams.
2 List and explain the 10 key challenges faced by group and team members.
3 Describe the five steps of team development.
4 List the five team dysfunctions and describe one managing tip for each of the dysfunction.

Note: Answers to the review questions are located in the Appendix.

Notes

* Saint-Exupéry, Antoine de. (1986). *Wartime writings 1939–1944* (trans. Norah Purcell). New York: Harcourt Brace Jovanovich.
1. Kozlowski, W. J., & Ilgen, D. R. (2006). Enhancing the effectiveness of work groups and teams. *Psychological Science in the Public Interest, Association for Psychological Science, 27*(3), 77–124.
2. Kozlowski.
3. Daft, R. L. (2012). *Management* (10th ed.). Mason, OH: South-Western Cengage Learning.
4. Bovee, C. L., & Thill, J. V. (2012). *Business communication today*. Boston, MA: Pearson.
5. The Atlanta Consulting Group, Inc. (1994). 1600 Parkwood Circle/Suite 200, Atlanta, Georgia 30339.
6. Bohlander, K. M. H. Predictor variables of constructive and destructive conflict behavior. Allied Academies International Conference. *Proceedings of the Academy of Organizational Culture, Communications and Conflict: Vol. 15/2*, 2–6.
7. Thomas, K. W., & Kilmann, R. H. (1974–2009). *Thomas-Kilmann conflict mode instrument*. Mountain View, CA: CPP.

8. Billikopf, G. (2003). Conflict Management Skills. Labor Management in Agriculture: Cultivating Personal Productivity. University of California: Regents of the University of California. Retrieved from http://www.cnr.berkeley.edu/ucce50/ag-labor/7labor/13.pdf

9. Murphy, E. C. (2009). Beyond accountability. *Leadership Excellence*, *26*(9), 14.

10. Fuqua, D. R., & Newman, J. L. (2002). *Consulting Psychology Journal: Practice and Research*, *54*(2), 131–140.

11. Martin, J. (1999, April). Building morale keeps employee spirits high in tough times. *HR Focus*, *76*(4), 9–10. Retrieved from ABI/INFORM Global. (Document ID: 40162636).

12. Anderson, S. A. (1997, July). Morale boosters—Humor in the workplace. *The Armed Forces Comptroller*, *42*(3), 34–35. Retrieved from Accounting & Tax Periodicals. (Document ID: 21734992).

13. Robbins, S. P., & Hunsaker, P. L. (2012). *Training in Interpersonal Skills* (6th ed.). Upper Saddle River, NJ: Prentice Hall.

14. Robbins & Hunsaker.

15. Wilson, D. (2010, January). "What price respect"—Exploring the notion of respect in a 21st century global learning environment. *Contemporary Issues in Education Research*, *3*(1), 95.

16. Yoest, J. (2006). Respect: The ultimate business etiquette. *Small Business Trends*. Retrieved from http://smallbixtrends.com/2006/10/respect-the-ultimate-business-etiquette.html

17. Gibson, J. L., Ivancevich, J. M., Donnelly, J. H. & Konopaske, R. (2009). *Organizations: Behavior, structure, processes* (13th ed.). New York: NY: McGraw-Hill/Irwin.

18. Gibson et al.

19. Gibson et al.

20. Gibson et al.

21. Thompson, L. L. (2004). Making the team: A guide for managers (2nd ed.). Upper Saddle River, NJ: Prentice Hall.

Communication Competency

Social Networks and Communicating Effectively in the Team Environment

If you can't explain it simply, you don't understand it well enough.

—Albert Einstein

Introduction

Previous chapters focus on the components that make working in a group or team more effective and efficient than working individually. In Chapter 5, the content is about the importance of communication and how communication affects every aspect of teamwork. It has been said that communication is the circulatory system of every interaction we experience, and this concept is of particular importance in team experiences. Communication is the process through which things get done among groups, teams and organizations.

Chapter 5 Competencies

The purpose of this chapter is to help you:
- Reflect on what you already know about the communication process.
- Learn fundamental communication process and model principles.
- Apply communication principles to team communication practices.
- Assess social networking strategies in the context of the team environment.

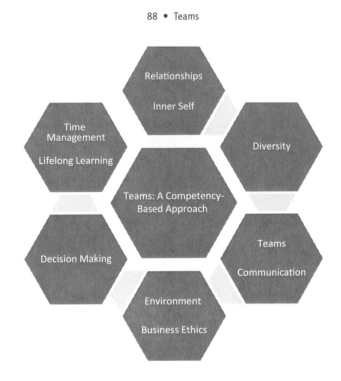

Figure 5.1

We communicate continuously with our words, body language, written messages and other symbols. Sometimes our lack of communication sends a message as well. The word *communication* comes from the Latin verb *communicare*, which means to inform, participate or share. With time, the use of the word has come to refer to the transfer of intangible or abstract things.[1] Communication includes a wide variety of channels, methods and audiences. Yet, all communication is represented by a systematic sequence of events. The basic process of all communication includes predetermined expectations of desired outcomes of events. The implication in this basic description is that one can send a message with the intent of receiving something in return. However, a sender should understand that the process includes the interpretation of the message by the receiver of the message, and therefore the possibility of the receiver hearing something different to what the sender expected. For example, the initiator of a message might say, "Please complete the assignment as soon as possible." Unless the intended receiver of the message asks for clarification or feedback, the interpretation of "as soon as possible" might range from "now" to "whenever I have time." No effective communication process is linear; it should be a continuous, iterative process.

The Communication Process

Figure 5.2

The classic communication process is based on the assumption that there is a common understanding between the sender of information and the receiver of the information. Effective communication is dependent on the transmission of a common understanding from the sender to the receiver.[2] Effective communication must be a two-way exchange.

Exercise: Test Your Communication Process Knowledge

The following chart illustrates an example of how the communication process can help to simplify and clarify messages in a step by step format.

Table 5.1

Process Step	Example	Process Meaning
Sender	A member of the group wants to meet to discuss a new idea.	Who is the person initiating communication?
Message	The group member wants to meet as soon as possible.	What is the communicator saying?
Medium	The group member sent an e-mail.	How is the communicator sending the message?
Receiver	The group member in charge of meeting schedules.	To whom is the message being sent?
Feedback	The receiver will check the schedule and send out notices after replying to the person who sent the request.	What effect does the message create?

Use the following chart to practice using the communication process by completing the blanks in the Example section of the chart.

Table 5.2

Process Step	Example	Process Meaning
Sender		Who is the person initiating communication?
Message		What is the communicator saying?
Medium		How is the communicator sending the message?
Receiver		To whom is the message being sent?
Feedback		What effect does the message create?

This simplification of the communication process is critical to understanding and improving the impact of each message. This not only makes communication more effective but also makes communication more efficient.

If only communication was that simple. In addition to the communication process, one needs to consider the environment in which all communication takes place. Typically, all communication has to maneuver through many distractions, barriers and what is usually referred to as noise. Noise includes communication distractions with both tangible and intangible characteristics. Tangible distractions include people, phones ringing, door bells sounding and so on. Intangible distractions include being tired, lack of sleep, feeling overwhelmed, and other personal setbacks such as divorce, death in the family and so on.

Many of the theories and models about communication in the world of work are based on the research of Shannon, Weaver and Schramm, who began researching communication in 1948 with their classic communication model.[3] This communication model evolved from the early works of these researchers and continues to provide useful characteristics toward the understanding of the communication process.

Elements of the Communication Model

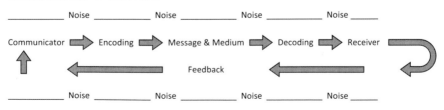

Figure 5.3

Communicator

The communicator is the person with the intention of creating a mutual understanding with someone else. As a communicator, this individual has an idea to share, a question to ask, a comment to make or some other type of purpose along these lines.

Example: When a phone rings, someone (a communicator) is attempting to send a message to someone else (a receiver). Noise includes distractions surrounding the event. Examples of noise in this example could include such distractions as others talking in the background, a fire alarm, another phone ringing, and preoccupations in the mind of the communicator.

Encoding

The second phase of the communication model is encoding. Encoding is the process through which the communicator translates the idea or question that he/she wants to share with another person into a set of symbols to which the receiver can relate. Language is the most common form of encoding.

Example: In the same example, a phone call, the communicator selects language as the encoding form with which to convey the message. Examples of noise in this stage of communication include the possibility of having such a diverse work environment that the communicator and the receiver do not share the same native language.

Message and Medium

A message can be verbal or nonverbal. It is the result of the encoding process: the content of the communication activity.

Example: In the phone call example, the communicator chose a verbal message. Examples of noise that could affect the communication include people talking in the background or to the communicator, a loud vehicle that passes by and a sneeze or a coughing fit.

The medium is the selected method of sending a message. A selected medium can include a choice from many available ways of sending a message depending on the impact that the communicator wishes to make. Mediums include face-to-face communication, e-mail, text, posters, bulletins and so on.

Example: In the ongoing example, the medium chosen is the phone. Noise, at this stage includes connectivity issues, weak batteries, no reception and unpaid phone bills.

Decoding

The decoding stage consists of the receiver's interpretation of the message sent by the communicator.

Example: Decoding noise includes any of the examples stated previously. In addition there is the possibility of the receiver missing the sender's phone call. Other variables come into play if the message is either not received at all or received via voice mail.

Receiver

The receiver is the individual who receives the communicator's message.

Example: Noise at the receiver's end of the communication includes all of the examples already listed. In addition, the receiver could be immersed in other tasks, distracted by personal problems or not interested in the communicator's message for a number of other reasons.

Feedback

Feedback is the process that helps the receiver to respond to the communicator. This critical phase of the communication models allows the communicator to determine the effectiveness of the message that was sent to the receiver.

Example: Ideally, once the receiver responds to the communicator, the process begins again to further clarify the message. Noise can interfere at this stage as well, for all of the same reasons stated in the previous examples. Other equally important examples of noise might include personality differences, emotions, conflict and physical illness.

Noise

Noise includes all of the environmental factors that can distort the message at every stage of the communication model/process. Noise includes time constraints, language barriers, misinterpretations and all of the examples included at each stage of the communication process.

The communication process and the communication model serve to set the foundation for all types of communication. These concepts are of particular importance in conducting business between individuals and among groups/teams. One-on one communication, although potentially complicated, tends to be easier to analyze in terms of its effectiveness. Since one-on-one communication is between two individuals, the potential for distractions and misinterpretations is limited compared to communication with more than one person. For example, in groups and teams, communication needs to occur among all of the members of the group. The number of individuals involved alone tends to introduce more noise into the conversations whether it is verbal, nonverbal, written and so on.

Project management professionals attribute success in managing teams to a formula that helps them determine the complexity of communication in all teamwork. The premise for the formula is based on years of research and experience that has led them to assert that the ultimate success or failure of teamwork is dependent on one factor: communication. The formula these project managers use for determining effective communication among the team is $N(N - 1)/2$; where N is equal to the number of team members involved in a given project.[4] The formula gives the communicator a number that equals the number of communication channels needed in order to make certain that each team member received the intended information. A communication channel is the path through which information passes between two individuals.

In a group or team of two participants, $N = 2$, and $2(2-1)/2 = 1$. The result of working the equation, the number one, indicates that effective communication should be disseminated through at least one channel between the two team members. A group of three participants effective communication calls for $3(3-1)/2 = 3$, or three channels of communication. In one more example, a group of 4 calls for $4(4-1)/2$, or six channels of communication. Clearly, the impact of adding one more person to a group of three increases the channels of communication significantly or twice as many channels.

The essence of analyzing the communication process is to avoid taking communication for granted. Most people tend to take the communication process for granted for the simple reason that talking is something they have done since an early age. However, talking is not the same as communication. Leigh Thompson, in her research on teams and teamwork, found that most

Table 5.3 Channels of Communication

Number of Team Members	Number of Channels of Communication
2	1 or $\quad$ A $\longleftrightarrow$ B
3	3 or $\quad$ A $\longleftrightarrow$ B C
4	6 or $\quad$ A $\longleftrightarrow$ B C $\longleftrightarrow$ D

groups are comprised of a selected few people who tend to do all of the talking. Thompson found examples that revealed the following:

- In a group of four people, two people do over 70% of the talking.
- In a group of six people, three people do over 86% of the talking.
- In a group of eight people, three people do over 77% of the talking.[5]

The significance of Thompson's findings is that those doing most of the talking might not be the ones with the most information for the group and/or team. Inevitably, the impact of talking instead of communicating will usually affect the team's productivity and effectiveness.

Exercise: This brief exercise is designed to help individuals who work in groups and teams understand how easy it is to misunderstand a message. This exercise is an adaptation of an exercise titled "How Soon Is Possible?"[6]

Read the word or phrase in the first column, and write a brief description of your meaning of the highlighted word in the column. After completing the list, compare your descriptions with another person in your class or group.

Example: The first column highlights a common word or phrase used in typical communication exchanges. The second column contains one person's interpretation of the highlighted word.

Table 5.4

Word/Phrase	Your Description
I want to meet with the team **frequently**.	**Frequently** means every week.
I need the report **soon**.	**Soon** means by the end of the week.
Please respond to my question when you have a **chance**.	**Chance** means as soon as possible.

Exercise: The first column highlights a common word or phrase used in typical communication exchanges. Fill in your interpretation of the highlighted word in the second column.

Table 5.5

Word/Phrase	Your Description
We need to talk **ASAP**.	**ASAP** means
Let's get together **soon**.	**Soon** means
The report is due **first thing** in the morning.	**First thing** means
It is **critical!**	**Critical** means
We cannot afford to miss this **opportunity!**	**Opportunity** means
This issue is a **show stopper!**	**Show stopper** means
I am **usually** late to meetings.	**Usually** means
I am **often** on time.	**Often** means
May I have a **minute** of your time?	**Minute** means
Let's do this on a **regular** basis.	**Regular** means

As you reflect on this exercise, consider the number of situations in which you have used these words/phrases and the numerous situations in which you might have interpreted the meaning of these words as they were transmitted to you. Words are the primary vehicle or symbol used for any type of communication. The meaning one associates with words depends on interpretation, past experiences, context and so many other factors. After all, the importance of effective communication can usually be best determined by the results of the intended communication more so than the response to the communication. It is best to prepare a message by thinking about the desired outcome;

one that speaks louder than the direct response. Clarity in communication is a good place to begin.

Now, compare your responses to a group or team member's responses. Discuss the importance of clear communication and the consequences of misinterpretations. Sometimes, misinterpretations can be readily cleared, and those involved can proceed with the business at hand. Unfortunately, unresolved misinterpretations can cause a domino effect with far-reaching consequences.

Historically, communicating with someone meant exactly that; from one person to another. Therefore, oral and written word became the most used channels of communication. Nonverbal communication was of utmost importance as well.[7] Fast forward to our current environment, where modern technology has shortened both distance and time to transform the ways in which we communicate. More than ever, one should consider H. Lasswell's classic description of the communication process, "Who says, what, in which channel, to whom and with what effect?"[8]

Communication Richness

Communication in the business environment, between individuals, groups, teams, management, customers and other individuals is conducted in a variety of ways. The communicator is in charge of selecting the media of sending a message by considering the richness of the selected method. Richness of communication refers to the likelihood of creating mutual understanding about a topic. In other words, how can an individual create a mutual understanding among others in the most efficient and effective way?

A medium that provides the most richness with the most realistic immediate feedback is face-to-face communication. Face-to-face communication is best used for important messages that are best relayed in person. Yet, face-to-face communication is at times impractical and impossible when you consider distances and time. Telephone and video communications are considered rich media, especially when face-to-face communication is not possible or perhaps expensive (travel). Telephone and video channels of communication offer ways to communicate efficiently with immediate feedback. In today's environment, texting is included in this category of high richness. A lower level of richness in communication media includes memos, letters, faxes and voice mail. Although these are not as effective as face-to-face, telephone and video, they offer options that keeps information flowing. Lower richness media provides an efficient venue for cost-effective ways to communicate routine information, announcements and other general messages that need to be distributed to a large audience. The lowest richness for communication purposes is that of wide distribution e-mails, bulletin boards, flyers, financial reports and other types of reports. These methods are best used for wide distribution of standardized information.

Exercise

Practice using the classic communication process and media richness. Each time you want to send a message to someone with whom you work, fill in the blanks in the following chart before sending the message to improve effectiveness in creating mutual understanding of the subject at hand.

Example: Each column heading describes one of the steps in the communication process. The following examples serve to illustrate two typical communications between team members.

Table 5.6

Who Says?	What?	To Whom?	Channel Richness?	Effect?
Team Member	Invite team members to lunch to celebrate a team accomplishment.	All team members.	Face-to-Face <u>Text</u> <u>Telephone</u>/Video Memo/Letter Voicemail Flyer Bulletin Board	Attend the event.
Team Member	Announce approval of the budget.	All team members and other stakeholders.	Face-to-Face Text Telephone/Video <u>Memo/Letter</u> Voicemail Flyer Bulletin Board	Inform others of a decision.

Exercise: Practice, practice, practice. Use the following chart to practice this brief analysis of any statement as it relates to the communication process. An ongoing exercise such as this one can make proper use of the components of the communication process more adaptable to daily communication.

Table 5.7

Who Says?	What?	To Whom?	Channel Richness?	Effect?
			Face to face	
			Text	
			Telephone/video	
			Memo/letter	
			Voice mail	
			Flyer	
			Bulletin board	

Social Networks as Communication Tools

Communication and collaboration between team members has improved in recent years, with the use of other technologies. Project management professionals use blogs and wikis to communicate with team members and other project stakeholders in real time. In one study, the researchers found the importance in balancing the amount of communication in teams is the most important factor with regard to innovation and productivity. Too much communication tends to lead to groupthink, while too little communication leads to isolation.[9]

The use of new and emerging technologies continues to improve efficiencies in communication that in turn enhance productivity for business groups and teams. Some of the most popular applications of technology in group and team communication to date include the following:

Social Networks

- Blogs—Blogs date back to the late 1990s to provide publically accessible journals on the Web.
- Podcast—A way to publish audio files to the Internet.
- RSS (Rich Site Summary)—A way of monitoring and distributing content that is sent to Web users.
- Screencast—A video file that contains audio.
- Social media—Programs that allow individuals to connect socially via computer.
  - Facebook—Launched in 2004, this Web site (online community) began as a place for college students to connect with other students via profiles, photos, videos and access to applications. Now, the Web site is open to anyone 13 years of age or older.

- MySpace—In 2003, this Web site began to help bands promote music and soon grew to include quite a general population. Individuals 14 years of age or older may join to share profiles that include personal information, interests, hobbies, educational background, photos and blogs.
- Classmates—This social networking site began in 1995. It serves to connect friends and acquaintances who attended school together from kindergarten through college.
- Friendster—In 2002, this Web site was launched to include friendships with anyone, not just past classmates.
- Twitter—This online service allows people to share quick (limited to 140 characters per message, or *tweet*) comments about everything and anything that is going on at the time. Twitter began in 2006.
- Tumblr—This is an online service founded in 2007 that allows users to share brief comments (blog), photos, quotes, links, music and videos. A popular feature offered by Tumblr is that it allows users to customize their blogs.
- LinkedIn—Founded in 2003. Similar to other social networking Web sites, LinkedIn is designed for business-oriented rather than personal networking. Members can search for jobs, and companies can search for employees. Also, LinkedIn provides a forum for continued contact between professional colleagues, such as coworkers and clients.
- hi5—Founded in 2003, this general networking site is popular in India, Mongolia, Thailand, Romania, Jamaica, Central Africa, Portugal and Latin America. It is not widely used in the United States.
- Badoo—Networking site, founded in 2006, popular in Europe and Latin America for meeting people and dating.
- Shelfari—Networking site for book lovers; founded in 2006.
- Migente—Top networking site in Latin America was founded in 2000.
- Orkut—2004 created by Google and popular in India and Brazil.
- StudiVZ—German version of Facebook.
- Business Networks
  - LinkedIn—Founded in 2003. Similar to other social networking Web sites, LinkedIn is designed for business-oriented rather than personal networking. Members can search for jobs and companies can search for employees. Also, LinkedIn provides a forum for continued contact between professional colleagues, such as coworkers and clients.

- Xing—In 2006, openBC, or open business club, changed names to Xing. This networking site helps keep track of business contacts; employers use this to fill job vacancies.
- Doostang—Founded in 2005, this networking site was created for young, top business professionals, to help them advance in their careers.
- Fast Pitch—This online business network was launched in 2006 for professional-to-professional networking and job seeking. It also is used in promoting different businesses.
- Ryze—Founded in 2001, helps people make connections and grow their networks, both business and social.
- Other Networks
  - Wiki—Founded in 1995, it is a collection of Web pages that can be edited by a group. Wiki is a Hawaiian term, *Wiki-Wiki*, meaning "very quick."
  - DoMyStuff—For those who need to hire someone to complete various tasks.[10]

Efficient use of these technologies depends on their use. It is important that team members agree to use these technologies and to learn how they work. One thing is clear—more and more successful teams are using technology for improved communication and, consequently, improved productivity. Make it a practice to keep up with the many changes occurring in the technology environment.

Computer mediated communication,[11] as well as numerous other applications of information technology, continues to make advances and contributions to aspects of communication in the business environment. Meanwhile, business environments are relying more and more on teams. Throughout Chapter 5 the benefits and challenges of effective communication were presented in the context of improving teamwork, productivity and effectiveness in the workplace by comparing communication to the human body's circulatory system. It is critical that team communications make wise use of technology while simultaneously staying in touch with the human side of communication. Positive and/or negative messages are quickly distributed throughout the members of a team, and it takes each member's awareness to maintain the intent of communication.

In Chapter 6, teamwork is presented in the context of the structure or environment surrounding the team. Of particular importance is the discussion of how organizational goals serve as the ultimate guidance and motivation for successful teams.

Review Questions

1 Write a message intended for a team member. In the message, use the communication process to structure the content as clearly as possible.

2 Describe the effects of noise on communication attempts based on the communication model.

3 Why is it important to analyze the relationship between communication channels and number of team members?

4 Describe communication richness and how it relates to teamwork.

5 Assess social networking strategies in the context of the team environment.

6 Conduct online research to find five current social networking sites. Are you currently using any of these sites for personal use? Describe the pros and cons of using these sites.

7 Conduct online research to find five current business networking sites. Which sites are you currently using? Describe the pros and cons of using these sites.

Note: Answers to the review questions are located in the Appendix.

Notes

* Einstein, A. (2013). The Biography Channel Web site. Retrieved from http://www.biography.com/people/albert-einstein-9285408

1. Bessonov, A. B. (2008). Communication processes: Role, place, content. *Scientific and Technical Information Processing, 35(4)*.

2. Gibson, J. L., Ivancevich, J. M., Donnelly, J. H. & Konopaske, R. (2009). *Organizations: Behavior, structure, processes* (13th ed.). Boston, MA: McGraw-Hill Irwin.

3. Gibson et. al.

4. Hodgkinson, J. (2009). *Communications is the key to project success*. Retrieved from www.asapm.org

5. Thompson, L. L. (2004). *Making the team: A guide for managers* (2nd ed.). Upper Saddle River, NJ: Pearson/Prentice Hall.

6. Withers, B., & Lewis, K. D. (2003). *The conflict and communication activity book*. New York, NY: AMACOM.

7. Bessonov.

8. Bessonov, p. 167.

9. Kratzer, R. T., Leenders, A. J., & Engelen, M. L. (2004, March). Stimulating the potential: Creative performance and communication in innovation teams, creativity and innovation management. *Creativity and Innovation Management, 13(1)*, pp. 63–71,

10. Mentrup, L. (2006, August). Social Network. *PM Network*, *20*(8), 26. ABI/IN-FORM Trade & Industry. Project Management Institute. Retrieved from www.pmi.org
11. Lowry, P. B., Romano, N. C., Jenkins, J. L. & Guthrie, R. W. (2009). The CMC interactivity model: How interactivity enhances communication quality and process satisfaction in lean-media groups. *Journal of Management Information Systems*, *26*(1), 159–200.

Environment Competency

Matching the Needs of the Organization

Innovation comes from people meeting up in the hallways or calling each other at 10:30 at night with a new idea, or because they realized something that shoots holes in how we've been thinking about a problem. It's ad hoc meetings of six people called by someone who thinks he has figured out the coolest new thing ever and who wants to know what other people think of his idea.

—**Steve Jobs***

Introduction

Successful organizations in the current changing business environment are increasingly dependent on teamwork to meet the challenges of market demands. In Chapter 5, communication was described as the circulatory system of teams and organizations in that effective links between people tend to create efficiencies in productivity. In this chapter, the importance of the structure or environment in which the team works will be described to give context to the team's work efforts and products.

In Chapter 6, the word environment is used to describe the surroundings of the workforce: the organization's structure, how it is designed and for what purpose. Also, the content of this chapter will include a description of how the organization's strategic goals are developed and supported through the structure to generate and sustain the work team's purpose.

Chapter 6 Competencies

The purpose of this chapter is to help you:

- Describe several types of organization structures found in today's work environment.
- Understand the relationship between organization structure and strategic goals.
- Explain the relationship between teamwork and organization structure in the workplace.
- Apply available resources that can be used to promote productivity in the team's environment.

Figure 6.1

Organization Structure and Design

An organization by definition is a social entity with goals, direction, coordinated systems and structures, all linked to the external environment. Whether for profit or nonprofit, organizations serve the following functions[1]:

- Coordinate resources for the achievement of organizational goals.
- Promote efficiencies in the production of products and services.
- Host innovations and creativity.
- Apply state of the art manufacturing and information technology.
- Navigate and influence the volatile environment.
- Provide value to all its stakeholders.
- Integrate the ongoing challenges presented by diversity, ethical dilemmas and the varied motivations of employees.

Exercise: The previous list provides functions served by organizations. Think about the companies in your community and those in which you work or have worked. What other functions can you add to the list?

1

2

3

Perhaps you added some functions that are unique to some organizations or functions that you have experienced through your work. The purpose of the brief exercise was to engage your thought processes in the topic of this chapter. Organizations are extremely complex, and it would take volumes to try to describe the intricacies that exist. The purpose of this chapter is to present an abbreviated overview of organizations in the context of teams and work groups.

Organizations consist of two dimensions: structural dimensions and contextual dimensions. These dimensions set the stage for how the organization maintains order while accomplishing goals. Structural dimensions include descriptions of the internal characteristics of the organization. Whether an organization is formal, specialized or centralized, the level of professionalism, personnel ratios and the chain of command are all included as characteristics of the structural dimension of an organization.

In formal organizations, documents exist that define and describe procedures, job descriptions, rules and policies. Formal institutions include large universities and corporations, such as those that deal in financial services. Small, family-owned businesses, on the other hand, tend to be more informal, with few written policies and procedures. Specialization within an organization is about whether employees focus on specific tasks or on general duties. Centralization refers to the decision-making level of the organization. When upper management reserves the decision making to their level of management only, the organization is described as centralized; when decision making drops to lower levels, it is said to be decentralized. Depending on the nature of the decision, some organizations can have centralized and decentralized decision-making roles throughout the levels of management and other employees. Professionalism in organizations is determined by the level of education and training among all employees. The personnel rations element of an organization's structural dimension describes the proportion of employees that work in the different departments.[2]

The contextual dimensions of an organization include the characteristics that describe the entire organization. Contextual characteristics include the organization's size, technology, culture, environment, goals and strategy. The size of an organization is usually determined by the number of employees. Technology refers to the way in which the members of the organization perform their jobs. The culture consists of the unique practices and internal environment that define how work is performed in a particular organization. Environment refers to everything that exists outside the organization's boundaries. Finally, the goals and strategy are the part of the contextual dimensions that make the organization different from other organizations regarding its purpose.[3]

Structural Dimensions

Organizational structure should be driven by an ongoing analysis of the organization's strategy and goals, along with an understanding of what the employees need for effective and efficient task completion. Generally, organizations deal with an external environment and an internal environment. The external and internal environments both affect strategy, goals, structure and productivity. The external environment includes two dimensions: the task environment and the general environment. In a nutshell, organizations take resources from the external environment and give products, goods and services back.

Environments That Affect Organizations[4]

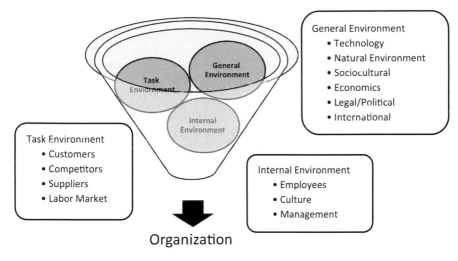

General Environment
- Technology
- Natural Environment
- Sociocultural
- Economics
- Legal/Political
- International

Task Environment
- Customers
- Competitors
- Suppliers
- Labor Market

Internal Environment
- Employees
- Culture
- Management

Organization

Figure 6.2

Overview of the Task Environment:

- Customers—those who use and/or depend on the organization's goods or services.
- Competitors—those organizations, in the same business, that sell goods or services to the same customers.
- Suppliers—those who provide raw materials for the organization's use in producing goods or providing services.
- Labor market—the people in the organization's environment that can be hired to do work for the organization.

Overview of the General Environment:

- Technology—includes scientific and technological advances that impact how the organization operates.
- Natural environment—includes all aspects of the environment that are natural, such as plants, animals, natural resources and so on.
- Sociocultural—includes the values, customs of the general population in the general environment.

- Economics—includes purchasing power, unemployment rate, interest rates and other aspects of the economy that surrounds the organization.
- Legal/political—includes local, state and federal regulations along with political activities that influence the organization's operations.
- International—includes events from other countries that affect the organization.

Overview of the Internal Environment:

- Employees—those who work for an organization.
- Culture—the set of patterns of behavior and shared values about how things are done in the organization.
- Management—those who run the organization.

Organization Structure and Strategic Goals

Organizations vary in structure, goals and purpose. They also range in size from multinational corporations to family-owned small businesses. Despite the many variations among organizations, they all have one thing in common: the people who work for the organization. In addition, organizations depend on the relationships their employees have with one another to help achieve organizational goals. Recent trends in management exist to improve relationships among employees by removing obstacles that in the past made collaboration and decision making complicated and time-consuming. One of the most successful changes in structuring and organizing work is in the increased dependence on groups and teams from different departments or areas within the organization to work together on assignments. This flattening of organizations is designed to improve horizontal communication between employees to successfully and consistently respond to our changing world.[5]

The importance of organization structure is driven by the needs, goals and strategies of each department, function or process within the organization. The design of each organization is based on four primary factors: how the employees need to be grouped, based on their specialization or expertise; where employees need to work to best streamline their work and products; how management can best plan, organize, lead and control the work; and where the decision making needs to take place (centralized or decentralized) to best move the organization toward success. Organization structure is typically either vertical or horizontal in nature. The following are examples of each of these traditional organization structures.

Sample Structural Design (Vertical or Functional) Organizational Chart[6]

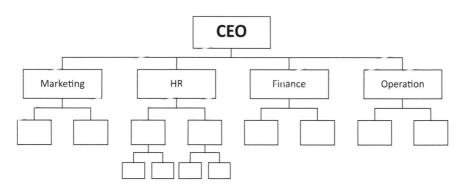

Figure 6.3

A vertical or functional structure consists of a limited number of corporate-level leaders with managers who report to them from the different functional levels. Functional levels are departments with employees who share similar knowledge, skills and abilities. The functional departments also share similar resources.

Functional structures, also associated with the mechanistic model, support the type of organizations that specialize in certain products or services. The functional structure design facilitates sharing of the organization's resources in one area of the company. The potential drawback of a functional structure is that communication and collaboration between functional areas can be challenging. Since departments focus on their area of specialization, there is no structural foundation for cross communication and sharing of ideas. Corporate level concerns include making sure that departmental initiatives ultimately support corporate-level business strategies.[7]

Horizontal structures, also supported by the organic model of organizational design, are significantly different than vertical structures. Horizontal structures are designed to support flexibility and development with few rules and procedures, decentralized authority and low levels of specialization. The flexibility of horizontal structures helps organizations adapt quickly to changing environments and their demands on products and services.[8]

Comparison of Mechanistic and Organic Models[9]

Table 6.1 Characteristics of the Mechanistic Model

Environment	*Relatively Stable*
Task differentiation	Not usually
Integration	Low integration between departments and functional areas; low dependency.
Decision making	Centralized
Standardization/formalization	High standardization with high formalization

Table 6.2 Characteristics of the Organic Model

Environment	*Relatively Dynamic and Uncertain*
Task differentiation	Much differentiation to adapt quickly to change
Integration	Tight integration to facilitate communication and information sharing
Decision making	Decentralized
Standardization/formalization	Minimal

Some organizations, depending on their size, purpose and locations, choose to combine mechanistic and organic structures into a matrix structure. The matrix approach helps staff from different functional and divisional areas to improve horizontal communication, coordination and information sharing. Inherent in this approach is the creation of two lines of authority and, ultimately, a least two bosses for each product or division. The success of the matrix approach is highly dependent on the interpersonal skills of those in supervisory positions. If this challenge is met, the benefits of this combined approach can include the advantages of each structure.

Sample Matrix Structure[10]

Globalization effects are causing the business environment to operate in a world without borders. Highly structured organizations are looking into

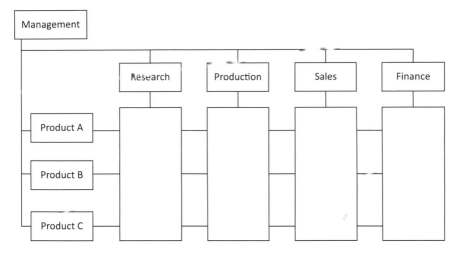

Figure 6.4

lost opportunities due to their less fluid networking environments and have begun to utilize the benefits of coordination and collaboration supported by horizontal structures. The most successful organizations in today's environment are utilizing virtual structures and subcontracting major functions to other companies. The strength of this vertical model is that it leaves the company free to concentrate on their expertise while hiring other companies to perform peripheral duties.

Virtual organizations, while appropriate and necessary in today's fast-paced environment, require a special way of viewing the environment. According to Scott M. Preston, in his research on virtual organizational processes, virtual organizations must pay attention to four key characteristics of this type of organization: complimenting competencies among the partners, high use of telecommunications, timeliness and trust between the partners.[11]

The International Center for Communications at San Diego State University created an Implementation Guide to help California communities adapt to the current business environment. The guide, Smart Communities, includes the following pros and cons of virtual organizations:[12]

Advantages of Virtual Organizations

- They are appropriate for "affinity groups," which may not be geographically contiguous.

- They are appropriate and tailored for short-term initiatives with clearly defined products or outcomes.
- Virtual organizations can be responsive to a rapidly changing environment.
- Virtual organizations have lower or nonexistent organizational overhead.
- They can help train key individuals who can the form the nucleus of a smart community.

Disadvantages of Virtual Organizations

- Virtual organizations have a higher dependency on technology for communication and coordination and are subject to the same limitations and problems inherent in these technologies.
- Virtual organizations may be unstable or difficult to manage.
- Because they are outside the normal institutional infrastructure, they may not necessarily have transformative effects on existing institutions.
- They are highly dependent on specific individuals and their interests.

Sample Virtual Structure

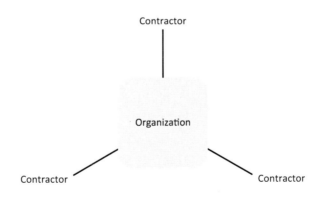

Figure 6.5

Contextual Dimensions

Organizations exist to provide products and services in an extremely competitive environment. In order to survive and even surpass their competitors, an organization's leaders must determine what they can do better than any other establishment, that is, their competitive advantage. A competitive advantage is achieved when an organization selects and implements a strategy that effectively uses the resources and processes supported by the structure of the organization. Strategic competitiveness is what a firm achieves when it creates a value-centered environment where everyone contributes.

Once the organization's leaders have studied the environments in which they intend to compete, the next step they take is to create a vision and mission for the organization. A vision statement gives the organization an ultimate goal for which to strive. A vision intends to capture the values and aspirations of everyone associated with the company in hopes of engaging all of the stakeholder's in the long-term strategy. It is the ultimate responsibility of the CEO to work with others on his staff to form the vision for the organization.

Examples of vision statements:

American Express: "We work hard every day to make American Express the world's most respected service brand."[13]

CVS/Caremark: "We strive to improve the quality of human life."[14]

Harley-Davidson USA: "We fulfill dreams inspired by the many roads of the world by providing remarkable motorcycles and extraordinary customer experiences. We fuel the passion for freedom in our customers to express their own identity."[15]

Macy's, Inc.: "Macy's, Inc. is a premier national Omni channel retailer with iconic brands that each operates outstanding stores and dynamic online sites. Both Macy's and Bloomingdale's are known worldwide, and each has its own unique identity and customer focus."[16]

McGraw-Hill: "Economic growth and job creation. 21st century skills. Greater transparency. That's our vision for this new decade. It is a vision for creating a smarter, better world—one where individuals, markets and countries have the knowledge and insights they need to develop and grow. In the pages that follow, we share the stories of how we at McGraw-Hill are laying the foundation for that future today."[17]

The mission statement is another important part of the company's strategy because it clearly identifies the business in which the organization will compete and the customers it will serve. Since the mission of the organization involves the market and customers, the CEO usually involves more of his or her upper and middle-level management in forming the mission statement. Some organizations refer to their mission in terms of their values and operating principles, as well.[18]

Examples of mission statements:

American Express: "We aim to provide products, services, benefits and rewards that deliver more value than any competitor. We focus on managing our business as efficiently as possible to continually improve the quality of our service and invest in growth. American Express has one of the world's most trusted brands. We strive to always provide the world-class service and personal recognition that our customers expect from us."[19]

CVS/Caremark: "We provide expert care and innovative solutions in pharmacy and health care that are effective and easy for our customers."[20]

Harley Davidson USA: "We ride with our customers and apply this deep connection in every market we serve to create superior value for all of our stakeholders."[21]

Macy's, Inc.: "Macy's, Inc. clearly recognizes that the customer is paramount and that all actions and strategies must be directed toward providing a localized merchandise offering and shopping experience to targeted consumers through dynamic department stores and online sites. Aggressive implementation of the company's customer-centric strategies by a talented, experienced organization will provide Macy's, Inc.'s, department stores with an important competitive edge. Macy's, Inc., is committed to open and honest communications with employees, shareholders, vendors, customers, financial analysts and the news media. The company seeks to be proactive in sharing information and in keeping these key stakeholder groups up-to-date on important and material developments. At Macy's, Inc., our greatest strength lies in the skill, judgment and talent of our people. Every day a production of enormous magnitude takes place on our selling floors and behind the scenes, where our people bring the company's strategic goals to life. Our priority of attracting, retaining and growing the most talented people in the retail industry has been and will continue to be our greatest advantage."[22]

McGraw-Hill: "As a global leader in financial services, education and business information, McGraw-Hill works with its partners and customers to help create a smarter, better world. The company's leading brands, such as Standard & Poor's, McGraw-Hill Education, Capital IQ, Platts and J. D. Power and Associates, promote the growth of the global economy, the improvement of business services and the advancement of education. In a world producing unprecedented quantities of data, the McGraw-Hill brands help society and businesses master this data with quality benchmarks, analysis and authoritative educational programs."[23]

Vision and mission statements are critical to an organization's success because they provide guidance, motivation and a set of standards with which to measure progress. It is every employee's responsibility to achieve organizational goals with efficiency and effectiveness. Efficiency is measured by the amount of resources used by the organization to achieve its goals. Effectiveness refers to how well the organization's goals are met.[24]

Organizations, in general, have numerous ways to measure and improve their efficiency primarily by using information technology. It is safe to say that efficiency can be addressed in a quantitative fashion. Effectiveness can be difficult to assess; it is a qualitative issue because it often depends on the expectations of the organization's stakeholders. A stakeholder is any group, inside or outside of the organization, who has a vested interest in the organization's outcomes. The following chart serves to illustrate how an organization's major stakeholders and what they expect from the organization can create numerous sets of expectations from one entity.

Stakeholder Groups and Their Expectations[25]

Table 6.3

Customers	Quality, Service, Value
Community	Support of community
Owners/stockholders	Profits
Creditors	Financial stability
Suppliers	Revenue
Government	Follow laws; fair competition
Union	Pay; Benefits
Management	Efficiency; effectiveness
Employees	Job satisfaction; pay

Although at first glance it seems like everyone wants the same results from the organization, the actual satisfaction level of each group is a much more difficult dilemma for the organization.

Strategic Goals and Team Goals

The work performed by teams and groups within an organization is composed of tasks that are of strategic importance to the organization. Project teams, especially, serve to improve horizontal communication throughout the organization. Trends in organizational design over the past decades have increasingly resulted in the development and implementation of teams.

The traditional or vertical structure of organizations, although great for providing controls, poses far too many challenges in efficiencies and effectiveness to the organization's success. The organizations that have embraced teamwork are able to profit from delegation of authority, quicker responses to the changing environment, and empowerment of those employees in lower levels to make their own decisions.

Organizations, in general, use two types of teams in achieving strategic goals. One type of team is the cross-functional team. Members of cross-functional teams usually continue to report to their functional department while also reporting to the team to which they are assigned. This approach usually works best for implementing change throughout the organization or for new product development.

Permanent teams, the other type of team approach, also focus on information sharing and communication. The difference between permanent teams and cross-functional teams is that permanent teams stay together to focus on specific tasks. These teams consist of members who have the knowledge, skills, abilities and authority to manage their own work.

Cross-functional teams and permanent teams are two high-level descriptions of how members of an organization work in the context of organizational design. More detailed information on teams is included in Chapter 4.

Review Questions

1 Define the term *organization* and describe five functions served by an organization.
2 Name and describe the two primary dimensions of an organization.
3 What are the three environments and their components that affect an organization's activities?
4 Why is an organization's structure important?

5 Explain the contextual dimensions of an organization.

6 Why are stakeholders critical to an organization's success?

7 What is the relationship between team goals and organizational goals?

Note: Answers to the review questions are located in the Appendix.

Notes

* Jobs, S. (1998). *BusinessWeek* interview. Retrieved from http://abcnews.go.com/ Technology/steve-jobs-death-20-best-quotes/story?id=14681795#2

1. Daft, R. L. (2010). *Organization theory and design* (10th ed.). Mason, OH: Southwestern Cengage Learning.

2. Daft, R. L.

3. Daft, R. L.

4. Daft, R. L.

5. Daft, R. L., ibid.

6. Nondhichakorn, A. N. (n.d.). Organization and management: Vertical organizational chart. Retrieved from http://www.bing.com/images/search?q=Organizati onal+Structure+And+Design&FORM=RESTAB

7. Hitt, M. A., Ireland, R. D. & Hoskisson, R. E. (2007). Strategic management (7th ed.). Mason, OH: Southwestern Cengage Learning.

8. Gibson, J. L., Ivancevich, J. M., Donnelly, J. H. & Konopaske, R. (2009). *Organizations: Behavior, structure, processes* (13th ed.). Boston, MA: McGraw-Hill Irwin.

9. BusinessMate.org. (2012, February 11). Mechanistic vs. Organic Organizational Structure (Contingency Theory). Retrieved from www.businessmate.org/Article

10. Satalkar, B. (2011, June 21). *Matrix organizational chart*. Retrieved from http://www.buzzle.com/articles/matrix-organizational-chart.html

11. Preston, S. M. (n.d.). Virtual organization as process: Integrating cognitive and social structure across time and space. Retrieved from http://ryan-brian-tute 1hbm370.blogspot.com/

12. Smart Communities Implementation Guide. (n.d.) How California's communities can thrive in the digital age [Web site]. Retrieved from http://www.smart communities.org/guide/index.html

13. McSween, D. (2010, December 4). *Get inspiration from these 10 famous vision statements*. Retrieved from http://www.brighthub.com/office/entrepreneurs/ar ticles/98189.aspx

14. American Express. (n.d.). Vision statement. Retrieved from http://about.ameri canexpress.com/oc/whoweare/

15. CVS-Caremark. (n.d.). Vision statement. Retrieved from http://info.cvscare mark.com/our-company/our-culture/vision-mission-values

16. Harley-Davidson. (n.d.). Vision statement. Retrieved from www.harley-david son.com/

17. Macy's. (n.d.). Vision statement. Retrieved from http://www.macysinc.com/ AboutUs/Vision/default.aspx

18. McGraw-Hill. (n.d.). Vision statement. Retrieved from http://www.mcgraw-hill.com/about/annual_report/ar2009.pdf

19. American Express.

20. CVS/Caremark.

21. Harley-Davidson.

22. Macy's.

23. McGraw-Hill.

24. Hitt, M.A., Ireland, R.D. & Hoskisson, R.E. (2007). Strategic management (7th ed.). Mason, OH: Southwestern Cengage Learning.

25. Daft, R.L.

Business Ethics and Social Responsibility

Competency

Sustainability in Today's Workplace

In the long run, we shape our lives, and we shape ourselves. The process never ends until we die. And the choices we make are ultimately our own responsibility.

—Eleanor Roosevelt[*]

Introduction

Why do individuals engage in unethical behavior? The events of question-able business practices in the recent past provide plenty of material for discussion and study. Textbooks and other literature in the business environment have seen a revival of ethics education and training that addresses the mishaps of WorldCom, Enron, Lehman Brothers and others. The renewed emphasis on business ethics centers on themes that include traditional topics from morals and values to a new emphasis on courage and accountability.[1]

In this chapter, ethics principles and practices are presented to introduce the topics in the context of a business environment supported by work teams. Ethics are ethics; yet, it is important to blend these concepts into the business environment where daily decisions are based on a continuum that includes all considerations from legal statutes to free choice. Ethics principles, ethical thinking and ethical decision making can serve as the stronghold for all business endeavors. The concepts of social responsibility and sustainability will add substance to this study of ethics in the business environment.

Chapter 7 Competencies

The purpose of this chapter is to help you:

- Review ethics principles and practices in business.
- Describe the relationship between ethics, the law and free choice.
- Understand the principles of social responsibility.
- Define sustainability and why it is important.
- Apply ethics principles to establishing an ethical environment.

Figure 7.1

Ethics Principles and Practices in Business

Ethics is, simply stated, about decisions and behavior with regard to right and wrong—as individuals, in groups and teams, within organizations and within society in general. Business ethics, also simply stated, is about the decisions we make and how we behave with regard to what is right and wrong as business individuals, in business groups and teams, within business organizations and within society in general.

Kirk Hanson, the executive director of the Markula Center for Applied Ethics, at Santa Clara University, suggests five ways to think about ethics. He refers to these principles as "traditions with practical application"[2] These are Hanson's five ways to think about ethics:

- Is the proposed behavior promoting the greatest good?
- Is the proposed behavior honoring the legitimate rights/human rights of individuals and groups?
- Will all parties be treated fairly?
- Is the behavior in line with accepted/traditional virtues?
- Is the common good adequately served?

The following four tables serve to illustrate how the five criteria are used to analyze an event in terms of Hanson's five ways to think about ethics.

Example: Individual behavior—You are an employee of a major corporation, and you sure could use an additional day of vacation. However, you only have a limited number of vacation days available for use. You decide to take the additional day by calling in and telling your boss you are sick.

Table 7.1

Behavior: Yes or No	Criteria
No	Is the proposed behavior promoting the greatest good?
No	Is the proposed behavior honoring the legitimate rights/ human rights of individuals and groups?
No	Will all parties be treated fairly?
No	Is the behavior in line with accepted and/or traditional virtues?
No	Is the common good adequately served?

Analysis of ethical dilemma: Based on the five criteria of ethical thinking, the proposed behavior described above is not ethically sound.

Example: Group behavior—You are working in a team, and your project is due in two days. Most of the work has been completed with the exception of one report missing from a team member who had to go out of town on a family emergency. You and your group decide to submit the deliverables for the project anyway since no one will notice the missing data.

Table 7.2

Behavior: Yes or No	Criteria
No	Is the proposed behavior promoting the greatest good?
No	Is the proposed behavior honoring the legitimate rights/ human rights of individuals and groups?
No	Will all parties be treated fairly?
No	Is the behavior in line with accepted and/or traditional virtues?
No	Is the common good adequately served?

Analysis of ethical dilemma: Based on the five criteria of ethical thinking, the proposed behavior described above is not ethically sound.

Example: Business organization—Your employer's senior management is meeting to determine the effects of downsizing on the organization's personnel. Lay-offs are inevitable; yet, they decide to hold off on any announcements to avoid unnecessary turmoil during the time leading up to the official announcements.

Table 7.3

Behavior: Yes or No	Criteria
No	Is the proposed behavior promoting the greatest good?
No	Is the proposed behavior honoring the legitimate rights/ human rights of individuals and groups?
No	Will all parties be treated fairly?
No	Is the behavior in line with accepted and/or traditional virtues?
No	Is the common good adequately served?

Analysis of ethical dilemma: Based on the five criteria of ethical thinking, the proposed behavior described above is not ethically sound.

Example: Corporate social responsibility—A local company provides its employees with paid time off so they can spend one day a month on volunteer work building houses with Habitat for Humanity.

Table 7.4

Behavior: Yes or No	Criteria
Yes	Is the proposed behavior promoting the greatest good?
Yes	Is the proposed behavior honoring the legitimate rights/ human rights of individuals and groups?
Yes	Will all parties be treated fairly?
Yes	Is the behavior in line with accepted and/or traditional virtues?
Yes	Is the common good adequately served?

Analysis of ethical dilemma: Based on the five criteria of ethical thinking, the proposed behavior described previously is ethically sound.

The examples provide an opportunity to see how ethical thinking standards can apply to any and many situations. In the following exercise, provide your own example of an ethical dilemma, to determine how the criteria for ethical thinking might apply in other situations.

Exercise: Individual Behavior—

Analysis of ethical dilemma:

Table 7.5

Behavior: Yes or No	Criteria
	Is the proposed behavior promoting the greatest good?
	Is the proposed behavior honoring the legitimate rights/ human rights of individuals and groups?
	Will all parties be treated fairly?
	Is the behavior in line with accepted and/or traditional virtues?
	Is the common good adequately served?

Exercise: Group Behavior—

Table 7.6

Behavior: Yes or No	Criteria
	Is the proposed behavior promoting the greatest good?
	Is the proposed behavior honoring the legitimate rights/ human rights of individuals and groups?
	Will all parties be treated fairly?
	Is the behavior in line with accepted and/or traditional virtues?
	Is the common good adequately served?

Analysis of ethical dilemma:

Exercise: Business Organization

Table 7.7

Behavior: Yes or No	Criteria
	Is the proposed behavior promoting the greatest good?
	Is the proposed behavior honoring the legitimate rights/ human rights of individuals and groups?
	Will all parties be treated fairly?
	Is the behavior in line with accepted and/or traditional virtues?
	Is the common good adequately served?

Analysis of ethical dilemma:

Exercise: Corporate Social Responsibility—

Table 7.8

Behavior: Yes or No	Criteria
	Is the proposed behavior promoting the greatest good?
	Is the proposed behavior honoring the legitimate rights/ human rights of individuals and groups?
	Will all parties be treated fairly?
	Is the behavior in line with accepted and/or traditional virtues?
	Is the common good adequately served?

Analysis of ethical dilemma:

Ethical Dilemmas

A template does not truly exist when it comes to ethics. These are basic guidelines, and each situation should be handled on its own merits. Nevertheless, the five suggestions stated above give some structure to instill a sense of consistency for ethical decision making.

In the work environment, employees come from many different backgrounds, were raised with a variety of values and have a multitude of experiences upon which they draw to make daily decisions. These factors are only a few of the variables that make ethics difficult to define. Ethical dilemmas arise every day in personal, group and organization environments as seen in the examples provided above at the beginning of the exercises. An ethical dilemma is a situation in which right and wrong are difficult to identify, and all of the choices for resolution of the dilemma tend to have less than ultimate results.

A pending decision may create an ethical dilemma in one environment, and the same circumstance may be a common practice in another environment. A bribe, for example, can be illegal in one environment. Yet, in another environment bribes might be a common practice. In this example, the choices and behaviors range from what is legal to what is free choice. Experts in the study of ethics describe this range of choices in a continuum, from legal to free choice, with ethical decision making midway between the two extremes.[3]

Figure 7.2

According to Dr. Richard Daft, a management professor at Vanderbilt University, human behavior falls into the three categories described above: legal, ethical and personal or free will. The standards by which the behaviors are measured range from the laws of the jurisdiction to the choices of individuals. The standard for ethics, which lies somewhere between legal statutes and free choice, is based on morals, values and principles. Individuals who fail to recognize and use morals and values as a tool for making ethical decisions tend to see every situation as, "if it's not illegal, it must be ethical".[4]

Chart Illustrating Law, Ethics and Free Choice

Organizations use normative decision making standards for guiding employee ethical decision-making challenges. The normative approach is based on customs, rules and values. A number of approaches exist for the normative strategy. Some of the most common approaches in today's organizations include: utilitarianism, moral rights, justice, virtue and practical.[5]

Utilitarianism

Consideration for making a decision based on utilitarian ethics takes into account the effect a decision will have on all of the people involved. The ultimate best utilitarian solution is the one with the most benefits for most individuals, for the longest period of time. Examples of utilitarianism include such decisions as approval of a new drug, whether to invest in certain projects and whether to monitor employee's use of alcohol and tobacco.[6]

Use the utilitarian approach by considering the following steps[7]:

1 Analyze and identify the options with regard to possible ways of handling the decision.
2 Identify those who will be affected by each possible solution.
3 List the benefits and/or negative consequences for those affected by the solution.

4   Select the decision that generates the greatest amount of benefits for the largest amount of individuals while producing the least harm.

Moral Rights

The moral-rights approach to ethical decision making is based on the fundamental rights and liberties of human beings. In making decisions, the decision maker must not interfere with such rights as the right to privacy, the right of free consent, the right to the truth, the right not to be injured and the right to freedom of speech, to name a few. Examples of moral-rights decisions might include alerting employees about lay-offs, providing a safe work environment, keeping promises to employees and avoiding actions that interfere with employee's personal lives.[8]

Use the moral-rights approach by considering the following[9]:

1   Does the decision respect the moral rights of all stakeholders?
2   Any decision that violates the rights of individuals is wrong.

Justice

The justice approach to ethical decision making asserts that decisions must be based on such standards as equity, fairness and impartiality. In making decisions under the justice approach, individual treatment of employees should be based on procedures, rules and standards to avoid making arbitrarily different decisions. An example of a justice-based decision might be the case when someone who is not as qualified receives a promotion instead of someone with higher qualifications.[10]

Use of the justice or fairness approach to make ethical decisions calls for the following considerations:[11]

1   Is the decision fair?
2   Are all stakeholders treated fairly as a result of the decision?
3   Does the decision create discrimination?
4   Does the decision create favoritism?

Virtue

The virtue approach to ethical decision making is about "doing the right thing." A virtue approach to ethics is based on developing good characteristics such as kindness, generosity, courage and compassion. These characteristics, in turn, set the stage for virtuous practices in that an individual makes decisions that come natural because of the inherent virtues of that individual. An example of virtue ethics is to not lie.[12]

The virtue approach to making ethical decisions requires the decision maker to ask the following questions:[13]

1 What kind of person should I be?
2 What will help me develop the characteristics to become a virtuous person?
3 Does the decision show honesty, courage, compassion, generosity, fidelity, integrity, fairness, prudence and self-control?

Practical

Ethics presents a wide, gray area in decision making for individuals, groups and organizations. The practical approach is often used to make decisions in situations over which there are "disagreements about the disagreements" in how to decide the best alternative. The practical-approach decision considers criteria such as acceptance of a decision by other professionals, by the general population and by an individual's family. In other words, the decision-making process considers the test of all stakeholders instead of what is right or wrong. Some examples of the practical approach might include decisions that affect issues such as affordable health care, public safety and the legal system.[14]

The practical or common good approach to making ethical decisions requires the following considerations:[15]

1 Are social policies, customs and institutions beneficial to everyone who depends on them?
2 Does the decision support the common good of the community at large?
3 Does the decision promote the most desirable kind of community?
4 Does the decision support and promote the goals that members of the community have in common?

These sets of guidelines and approaches are but a few examples of how individuals, group members and members of organizations adapt to the changing environment. Ethical dilemmas vary as do values, virtues and circumstances. The guidelines serve to provide some structure so that ethical decisions can be somewhat consistent in the impact and consequences that follow these types of decisions. As organizations continue to embrace ethical decision making, the concept of sustainability continues to gain momentum as well. Sustainability is about generating benefits and gains for the current generation while protecting the environment for future generations.

Corporate Social Responsibility

Organizations establish their stance on differentiating right from wrong through corporate social responsibility (CSR) programs. CSR is the organization's commitment to make decisions that will benefit society as well as the organization.[16]

The primary model of CSR contains four domains of responsibility: economic, legal, ethical and philanthropic.[17] Together, the four criteria provide the social responsibility benchmarks for a company's level of response to CSR expectations.

Economic CSR

In the past, an organization's economic responsibility was limited to making a profit for the company and its stakeholders. A purely profit oriented approach is no longer acceptable in the United States, Canada and Europe in efforts to deter corruption in business dealings.[18]

Legal CSR

An organization's legal social responsibilities include adherence to local, state and federal laws. Some of the examples included in an organization's legal social responsibility include avoiding fraud, defective good, unnecessary services and inflated billing practices.

Ethical CSR

Ethical responsibilities of organizations include making ethical decisions, as described earlier in this chapter. An organization is described as ethical when its profits and successes do not occur at the expense of other organizations or individuals.

Philanthropic CSR

Philanthropic responsibility, also known as discretionary responsibility, is quantified by the organization's voluntary contributions. This is the highest level of corporate social responsibility in that it goes beyond legal and social expectation. The main purpose of philanthropic responsibility is to contribute to society by giving back to the immediate community.

Sustainability

Corporate responsibility can be summarized with one word: *sustainability*. Sustainability refers to how an organization strives for economic development and earnings in the current environment while taking into account the needs of future generations.[19]

In 1994, John Elkington, a British consultant who founded his business and named it SustainAbility, coined the phrase "the triple bottom line." Since the early 1990s, business people like Mr. Elkington have argued that a company's true measure of success should be based on more than the traditional bottom line of profit and loss. The triple bottom line, according to Elkington, consists of three "Ps": profit, people and planet. In addition to measuring an organization's financial standing, two other aspects need measuring as well: social responsibility and environmental responsibility. The result of measuring the three Ps can then be truly equated to an organization's balanced scorecard.[20]

Although the push for attention to the triple bottom line began with some enthusiasm and interest, it was followed by a decline in corporate social responsibility and economic chaos. There is now a resurgence of interest and support of corporate social responsibility. One example is the Global 100, which is an organization that began in 2005 with the purpose of identifying the top 100 most sustainable companies in the world. The criteria used by Global 100 include[21]:

1   Energy productivity
2   Greenhouse gas productivity
3   Water productivity
4   Waste productivity
5   Innovation capacity
6   Percentage taxes paid
7   CEO to average employee pay
8   Safety productivity
9   Employee turnover

10   Leadership diversity
11   Clean capitalism paylink

Renewed interest and participation in corporate social responsibility begins with senior management and affects every employee of the organization. Many studies are beginning to identify the struggles and successes of companies that are including the three Ps in strategic management planning and other initiatives.

Exercise for CSR/Sustainability:

Use your favorite Internet search engine to identify the characteristics of the following companies that make each of them corporate socially responsible entities. How are they practicing sustainability?

Example

Table 7.9

Company	Examples of corporate social responsibility and sustainable practices
General Electric	Ecomagination—GE's efforts to include innovative solutions to current environmental issues while achieving economic growth.[22]
IBM	Let's build a better planet—Smarter Buildings.[23]
Procter & Gamble	13th Annual Sustainability Report—numerous examples.[24]

Exercise:

Select three companies of your choice, and conduct a search online to determine the company's corporate social responsibility and/or sustainability efforts. Use the following chart to document your findings.

Table 7.10

Company	Examples of corporate social responsibility and sustainable practices.
1	
2	
3	

Exercise:

Reflect on the findings of your search for socially responsible companies. Did your search also reveal some companies lacking in socially responsible initiatives and practices? Compare the two types of companies. Which ones would you prefer to have as an employer?

Your comments:

Creating an Ethical Environment

Ethical dilemmas occur on a daily basis, in every environment and with varying results. Some ethical dilemmas go seemingly unnoticed, while others deliver power consequences. In successful organizations, the strategic-planning process includes goals and objectives designed to create and sustain an ethical environment. Individuals who are hired by organizations come from different parts of the world with varying sets of values and backgrounds. Setting goals and objectives for an ethical environment provides a set of norms for all employees. A general "to do" list of critical items for an ethical environment begins with the following[25]:

1   Establish an enforceable code of conduct
2   Initial and ongoing training
3   Regular communications
4   Anonymous reporting hotline
5   Enforcement/action
6   Reward employees that live the culture

Code of Conduct

Richard Thornburgh, a former U.S. Attorney General, said,

> Subordinates cannot be left to speculate as to the values of the organization. Top leadership must give forth clear and explicit signals, lest any confusion or uncertainty exist over what is and is not permissible conduct. To do otherwise allows informal and potentially subversive "codes of conduct" to be transmitted with a wink and a nod, and encourages an

inferior ethical system based on "going along to get along" or the notion that "everybody's doing it.[26]

A code of conduct serves as a guide and reference for all employees of an organization for making decisions about day to day activities. The code includes the company's mission, vision, values, principles and other standards of ethical and professional conduct. Responsible organizations use the code of conduct to encourage and enhance relationships between employees, the community and other stakeholders.[27]

The Ethics Resource Center offers the following tips for writing a code of conduct for an organization[28]:

1   Think in terms of values, beliefs and expectations rather than facts.
2   Keep it simple.
3   Be concise.
4   Use active voice rather than passive voice.
5   Give examples when appropriate.
6   Write so that others can understand—they are not experts in this area.
7   Do not attempt to write polished prose; keep updating your draft.
8   Read your work aloud to yourself.
9   Make your writing look easy to read.
10 Have others, especially your harshest critics, read what you have written.

Training

Initial and ongoing training are crucial in maintaining an ethical environment in every organization. Effective ethics training and education includes information that increases everyone's knowledge, instruction that enhances decision-making skills and case analysis that encourage ethical reasoning.[29] Training approaches vary from company to company. While most employees still prefer the classroom approach, companies are utilizing many approaches, from classroom training to a wide use of technology.

Does the organization where you work or have worked promote ethics training? Answer the following questions to analyze your work environment by selecting "yes" or "no":

1   I received ethics training when I was first hired.   Yes   No
2   Ethics training is conducted on a regular ongoing basis. Yes   No

3	I am aware of the company's values and policies.	Yes	No
4	The company's code of conduct and/or code of ethics is visible and available to all employees.	Yes	No
5	Management is supportive of ethics standards.	Yes	No
6	I have opportunities to contribute to ethic values.	Yes	No
7	Ethics is the responsibility of every employee.	Yes	No
8	I work for an ethical organization.	Yes	No

Review your answers. Any no answer presents a possible opportunity to develop or improve ethics in the work environment. The yes answers should also be reviewed for ongoing improvement opportunities.

Communication

Communication within an organization is composed of three formal channels: upward, downward and horizontal communication. Upward and downward communications are typically used in traditional, vertically structured organizations. Yet, many organizations in the current environment are also including horizontal communication to maintain fluidity between departments and levels within the organization. All three formal channels of communication are available for use in ethics training and education efforts within the organization.

Upward communications consist of the information that flows toward management. Most of the content of upward communications includes problems, performance reports, grievances, suggestions for improvement and financial information. Management uses this information as a listening tool for continuous improvement.

Downward communications help management send messages throughout the organization for the purpose of influencing the general employee population. Messages in downward communications include goals, strategies, instructions, procedures and performance feedback.

Horizontal communications occur laterally among coworkers and other peers. The main purpose of horizontal communication is for sharing information, requesting help and coordinating efforts.

Anonymous Reporting Hotline

In some organizations, management goes beyond policies and procedures in their efforts to encourage ethical practices. Employees are encouraged to report corporate wrongdoings by providing an internal anonymous reporting hotline. Employees who use the anonymous hotline can do so without jeopardizing their jobs and reputation with the organization.

Some incidents of corporate illegal or unethical practices are reported to outsiders, such as the media, politicians or regulatory agencies. This practice is known as whistle-blowing. Ethical organizations pursue avenues through which employees are encouraged to report incidents internally, to the organization's management or ethics office. However, external reporting, or whistle-blowing, consists of tremendous risks for the whistle-blower. Whistle-blowers are often viewed as employees who are disenchanted with the organization and want to cause trouble. Support and protection for whistle-blowers varies from state to state. The following chart contains a summary of the protection offered to whistle-blowers throughout the United States, as of 2005.[30]

Table 7.11 State Whistle-Blower Laws

State	*Covers*	*Provisions*
Alabama	state employees	State Employees Protection Act
Alaska	public employees	Prohibits employers from discharging, threatening or otherwise discriminating against an employee who reports on a matter of public concern.
Arizona	n/a	None
Arkansas	n/a	None
California	all employers	Similar to the provisions stated above.
Colorado	state & health care employees	Similar to the provisions stated above.
Connecticut	public & private employers	Similar to the provisions stated above.
Delaware	public employees	Similar to the provisions stated above.
DC	n/a	None
Florida	public & private employers	Similar to the provisions stated above.
Georgia	health workers	Similar to the provisions stated above.
Hawaii	private & public employers	Similar to the provisions stated above.
Idaho	n/a	None

(Continued)

Table 7.11 (Continued)

State	Covers	Provisions
Illinois	public employees	Similar to the provisions stated above.
Indiana	state employees	Similar to the provisions stated above.
Iowa	state employees	Similar to the provisions stated above.
Kansas	state employees	Similar to the provisions stated above.
Kentucky	state employees	Similar to the provisions stated above.
Louisiana	all employers	Similar to the provisions stated above.
Maine	public & private employers	Similar to the provisions stated above.
Maryland	public employees	Similar to the provisions stated above.
Massachusetts	any employer	Similar to the provisions stated above.
Michigan	all employers	Similar to the provisions stated above.
Minnesota	public & private employers	Similar to the provisions stated above.
Mississippi	n/a	None
Missouri	state employees	Similar to the provisions stated above.
Montana	n/a	None
Nebraska	private, public & union employees	Similar to the provisions stated above.
Nevada	n/a	None
New Hampshire	public and private employers	Similar to the provisions stated above.
New Jersey	public & private employers	The Conscientious Employee Protection Act (CEPA)
New Mexico	n/a	None
New York	public and private employers	Similar to the provisions stated above.
North Carolina	n/a	None
North Dakota	private employers	Similar to the provisions stated above.
Ohio	private & public employers	Similar to the provisions stated above.
Oklahoma	state employees	Similar to the provisions stated above.
Oregon	private & public employees	Similar to the provisions stated above.

(Continued)

Table 7.11 (Continued)

State	Covers	Provisions
Pennsylvania	public employers	Similar to the provisions stated above.
Rhode Island	public & private employers	Similar to the provisions stated above.
South Carolina	government employers	Similar to the provisions stated above.
South Dakota	n/a	None
Tennessee	public & private employees	Similar to the provisions stated above.
Texas	n/a	None
Utah	public employees	Similar to the provisions stated above.
Vermont	health care employees	Similar to the provisions stated above.
Virginia	public employees	Fraud and Abuse Whistle Blower Protection Act
Washington	state employees	Similar to the provisions stated above.
West Virginia	state employers	Similar to the provisions stated above.
Wisconsin	n/a	None
Wyoming	n/a	None

Enforcement

Written codes, frequent training and supportive communication are only messages that contain suggestions for proper behavior if enforcement is missing from the ethics program. Enforcement and action are necessary in order to avoid costly violations of ethics policies.

A study by the Ethics Resource Center found that "the rate of misconduct is cut by three-fourths at companies with strong ethical cultures, and reporting is doubled at companies with comprehensive ethics programs."[31]

Living the Culture

The steps in developing an ethical culture should include a reward system for employees that behave ethically. These employees, with their ethical behavior, serve as an example for others within the organization. Together with a written policy, training, communication and the ability to report unethical behavior, rewards for ethical behavior tend to complete the elements of an ethical culture.

Courage and Accountability

Establishing an ethical working environment provides the system, resources and the foundation for ethical behavior. Yet, the challenge that remains lies in encouraging employees to come forth with reports of unethical behavior. The more difficult areas to manage and measure are courage and accountability. Organizations provide incentives, and trends develop in time that support courage and accountability.

Everyone benefits from the commitment to an ethical environment. Documented evidence of the benefits includes less risk, less fraud, less litigation and happier employees. All of these benefits lead to an improved bottom line.[32]

In Chapter 8, Decision-Making Competency, the content will add another layer to the duties and responsibilities of individuals who work in groups and teams. While Chapter 7 offers concepts in support of business ethics and social responsibility, the chapter on decision making will focus on more of a hands-on approach to the steps in making consistently good day-to-day decisions in the work environment.

Review Questions

1 Discuss ethics principles and practices in business.
2 Why is it important to understand the relationship between ethics, the law and free choice?
3 Describe the principles of social responsibility. Why are these principles an important aspect of an organization's strategy?
4 Define sustainability and why it is important.
5 Apply ethics principles to establishing an ethical environment. Explain how to develop an ethical environment in the workplace.

Note: Answers to the review questions are located in the Appendix.

Notes

* Roosevelt, E. (1959). *Prospects of mankind with Eleanor Roosevelt* [Film transcript]. Retrieved from http://www.pbs.org/wgbh/americanexperience/features/bonus-video/eleanor-prospects-mankind/

1. Painter-Morland, M. (2006). Redefining accountability as relational responsiveness. *Journal of Business Ethics, 66*, 89–98.
2. Hanson, K. O. (2010), Five ways to think ethically [Video clip]. Retrieved from http://www.scu.edu/ethics/practicing/focusareas/business/introduction.html
3. Daft, R. L. (2012). *Management* (10th ed.). Mason, OH: South-Western Cengage Learning.
4. Daft, R. L.
5. Trevino, L. K., & Nelson, K. A. (2010). *Managing business ethics: Straight talk about how to do it right* (5th ed.). John Wiley & Sons.
6. Andre, C., & Velasques, M. Calculating Consequences: The Utilitarian Approach to Ethics. Retrieved on March 17, 2012 from http://www.scu.edu/ethics/publications/iie/v2n1/calculating.html
7. Williams, W. R. (n.d.). Ethics and law: Basic concepts, cases, and dilemmas. Retrieved from www.baruch.cuny.edu/. . . /documents/EthicsandLaw.doc
8. Velasquez, M. Andre, C., Shanks, T., & Meyer, S. J. (1996, Winter). Thinking ethically: A framework for moral decision making. *Ethics, 7*(1). Retrieved from http://www.scu.edu/ethics/practicing/decision/thinking.html
9. Williams, W. R.
10. Williams, W. R.
11. Williams, W. R.
12. Williams, W. R.
13. Velasquez, M., et al.
14. Hanson, K. O. (2010). Strategies for managing ethics [Video clip]. Retrieved from http://www.scu.edu/ethics/practicing/focusareas/business/introduction.html
15. Velasquez, M., et al.
16. Williams, W. R.
17. Daft, R. L.
18. Geva, A. (2008, March).Three models of corporate social responsibility: Interrelationships between theory, research and practice. *Business and Society Review, 113*(1), 1–41.
19. Daft, R. L.
20. Hindle, T. (2009, November 17). Triple bottom line: It consists of three Ps: Profit, people and planet. *The Economist.* Retrieved from http://www.economist.com/node/14301663
21. Global 100 Most Sustainable Corporations in the World. (n.d.). *Criteria and weights*. Retrieved from http://www.global100.org/methodology/criteria-a-weights.html
22. Ecomagination. (n.d.). General Electric Web site. Retrieved from http://www.ecomagination.com/paging-little-miss-muffet-farmers-maximize-energy-from-cheese-waste
23. Let's Build a Better Planet: Smarter Buildings. (n.d.). IBM Web site. Retrieved from http://www.ibm.com/smarterplanet/us/en/green_buildings/overview/index.html?re=CS1
24. 13th Annual Sustainability Report. (n.d.). Procter & Gamble Web site. Retrieved from http://www.pg.com/en_US/sustainability/index.shtml

25. Heaps, G. (2008, August 12). Six steps to creating an ethical culture: And the four benefits your business will enjoy. Version 3. *Knol.* Available from: http://knol.google.com/k/greg-heaps/six-steps-to-creating-an-ethical-culture/k6epi09pi77h/2

26. Ethics Resource Center. (2009, May 29). *Why have a code of conduct?* Retrieved from http://www.allegiance.com/library.php

27. Hughes, R. L., Ginnett, R. C., & Curphy, G. J. (2002). Leadership: Enhancing the lessons of experience (4th ed.). Boston, MA: McGraw-Hill Irwin.

28. Brown, J. (n.d.). *Ten writing tips for creating an effective code of conduct.* Ethics Resource Center. Retrieved from http://ethics.org/resource/ten-writing-tips-creating-effective-code-conduct

29. Menzel, D. C. (2009). Ethics Education and Training, Part 1. Public Integrity, Vol. 11 Issue 3, pp. 197–199.

30. National Conference of State Legislatures. (2010, November). *2005 state whistleblower laws.* Retrieved from http://www.ncsl.org/issues-research/labor/state-whistleblower-laws.aspx

31. Heaps, G.

32. Heaps, G.

Decision-Making Competency
Critical Thinking for Consistently Making Each Decision the Best Decision

We can't solve problems by using the same kind of thinking we used when we created them.

—Albert Einstein[*]

Introduction

Decisions are faced and made every day. Some decisions are easier to make than others; yet, all decisions have consequences. The purpose of including decision making in Chapter 8 is to provide some guidelines for consistent and effective decision-making practices. This chapter will include group

---

Chapter 8 Competencies

The purpose of this chapter is to help you:
- Analyze the decision-making process.
- Review basic decision-making alternatives.
- Determine the best decision-making alternative to use.
- Understand some decision-making pitfalls.

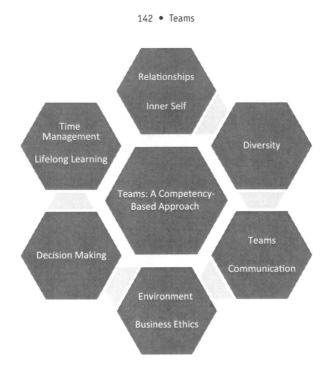

Figure 8.1

decision-making practices in addition to general comments from current research on this invaluable skill.

A practical approach to decision making might suggest three possible alternatives: ignore the issue, quickly get rid of the issue or address the issue through sound decision-making practices. While ignoring and disposing of the issue quickly tend to make the issue more complex, taking a structured decision-making approach can yield richer results.[1]

Consider, for example, the following scenario: A group of employees has been working on a task for the past few weeks, and they are preparing their first formal report. The team has expectations of publishing the report in a professional journal. One of the team members notices that portions of the report written by a team member sound familiar, and he suspects plagiarism. What should the reviewer of the report do? Should he ignore the issue, quickly get rid of the issue or address the issue through sound decision making?

The Decision-Making Process

Is decision making a pleasant experience or a dreaded chore? Sometimes, decision making can be both: a mixed experience, depending on the approach that is taken.

Exercise:

In the following spaces, list five decisions you made recently. Next to each decision, indicate if making the decision was a pleasant or unpleasant experience.

Table 8.1

Decision	Pleasant	Unpleasant
1		
2		
3		
4		
5		

Reflect on your answers to the exercise by answering the following questions for each decision listed previously.

1 Was the decision one that you make on a regular basis?
2 Was the decision easy to make?
3 Was it a difficult decision to make?
4 What factors made the decision a pleasant experience?
5 What factors made the decision an unpleasant experience?
6 What would you do differently?

The exercise and reflection provided are designed to help individuals begin to break down the decision-making process. Specifically, it is important to put decision making into the proper context; the decisions we have to face as individuals and as members of groups and teams.

So, how do you make decisions? Answer the following questions based on the results of the two previous exercises:

Exercise: How do you make decisions?

1 Do you consider the choices available to you at the time?
2 Do you think about decision making as an opportunity or a problem?
3 Do you wonder if you have all of the information you need to make the decision?
4 Are you the best individual to make the decision?
5 Are you a risk taker?
6 How do you handle ambiguity?
7 Do you have good instincts, and do you trust your instincts?

Think about a recent important decision you made. Perhaps you made a decision to change careers or decided to move to another city. How did you decide? What steps did you take? Read the following and circle five that best describe how you made your recent important decision.

Table 8.2

1 Logic	6 Instinct
2 Inner knowing	7 Prior knowledge
3 Data	8 Hunch
4 Felt it was the right decision	9 Reasoning
5 Facts	10 Feelings

The previous list identifies two types of decision-making preferences, linear and intuitive. The odd-numbered items describe a preference for a linear decision-making preference, while the even numbered items describe a preference for an intuitive decision-making style. Neither style is right nor wrong; they simply represent different preferences. Identifying all linear items or all intuitive items in this exercise can mean that you have a strong preference for one style over the other.[2]

Linear approaches to decision making are also referred to as the rational approach. This model of decision making describes the ideal way of making decisions because it includes thorough analysis of known information. In theory, the rational approach helps arrive at the best decisions for all of the parties involved. This model is preferred in the business environment because it tends to lead to the organization's economic interests. The four assumptions upon which this model is based include:[3]

1 Goals of the organization are known and accepted.
2 Information is known, and all alternatives with possible results are available.
3 Based on established criteria, decisions on which alternative to select are based on the best economic return to the company.
4 All decisions are based on logic, values and preferences that maximize the company's ability to reach organizational goals.

Intuitive approaches to decision making rely on the decision maker's years of knowledge, experience and practice in the work environment. The absence of time-consuming analysis typically found in the rational approach helps intuitive decision makers reach decisions quickly. Research in the field of decision making indicates that the best approach is to use a combination of both rational and intuitive decision-making practices.[4]

Simply stated, there are two basic situations in which decisions take place. One type of decision only requires the person making the decision. The second type of decision includes others as well. Even when working with others, as in a group or team, an individual might be faced with an individual or minority decision. Certain situations, such as time constraints or emergencies, could create a need for a quick decision made by one person. In group or team settings, there are two circumstances for decision making: majority opinion and consensus. In seeking a majority opinion, a decision is usually made by voting. If the situation calls for additional levels of commitment and support, it is best to reach consensus in the decision-making process.[5]

Consensus requires buy-in from the individuals who are going to be affected by the results of the decision. Although reaching consensus can be a time-consuming undertaking, the process can be streamlined with proper planning and applicable techniques. Proper planning can be as simple as giving the decision makers the information they need and a fair amount of time to consider their alternatives. One of the most useful techniques for quick consensus decision making is the nominal group technique. These are the eight steps for applying the nominal group technique:[6]

1   Clearly state the goal you need to achieve.
2   Make agreements about the decision-making process.
3   Generate ideas individually and privately. Each person writes down their ideas.
4   Take turns in sharing ideas and recording them without discussion.
5   Evaluate ideas in detail. Narrow the list to the top five ideas, and list evaluations with pros and cons.
6   Vote on the ideas by designating 5 points for a first choice, 3 points for a second choice and 1 point for a third choice.
7   Add the votes, and identify the first, second and third choices.
8   Check for consensus: Does everyone agree with the majority or at least, support the most popular choice?

Some decisions may be too complex for a simple process as the nominal group technique. One approach for complex decisions is to create a matrix with agreed upon criteria. The matrix can be used as step 6 in the nominal group technique steps. An example of a decision making matrix might include the following criteria:[7]

Table 8.3 Decision-Making Matrix

Decision	Importance	Cost	Difficulty	Value to Those Concerned	Total

Use scores of 1 to 5 per item, and per column; 1 = *worst* and 5 = *best.*

Typically, a decision-making opportunity occurs when a problem surfaces. A problem is defined as any situation in which the circumstances are below the established expectations. An opportunity is defined as an intervention that can increase accomplishments beyond the established expectations.

Effective decision making is associated with the successful completion of six steps. The steps in the decision-making process include:[8]

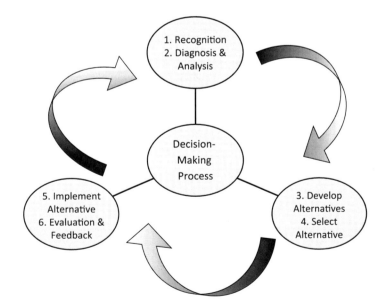

Figure 8.2

The Decision-Making Process: Step by Step

Table 8.4 Decision-Making Matrix

Decision-Making Step	*Activities*
1 Recognition	• Review goals • Are goals being accomplished? • If no, go to Step 2
2 Diagnosis	• What is the problem? • When did it occur? • Where did it occur? • How did it occur? • To whom did it occur? • Is the problem urgent? • Are the events connected? • Results of the analysis.
3 Develop Alternatives	• Identify solutions for the initial problem. • What needs to happen in order to turn the situation around? • Do not limit your number of alternatives. • Keep referring to Steps 1 & 2 when identifying alternatives.
4 Select Alternative	• Which alternative will yield the most substantive results? • Consider what risks are acceptable. • Consider both rational and intuitive decision making approaches. • Consider the resources needed. • Keep referring to Steps 1, 2 & 3 when selecting the alternative that best resolves the problem.
5 Implement Alternative	• Put the alternative into action. • Make use of available resources. • Communicate well and extensively. • Sell the alternative to all stakeholders.

(*Continued*)

Table 8.4 (Continued)

Decision-Making Step	Activities
6 Evaluation & Feedback	• Gather information once the alternative has been implemented.
	• Did the selected alternative create the change needed to solve the problem?
	• What is working well?
	• What is not working well?
	• Solicit feedback from stakeholders.
	• Do you need to start the decision-making process over again?

The decision making process is . . . a process. It is entirely possible that one alternative simply identifies another problem. Sometimes, the initial problem is too complex to correct with one attempt. Decision making is a learning process that requires astute observation, constant communication and effort from all of the parties involved. Do not give up on the first try!

Outcome-Directed Thinking

Decision-making practices will vary, depending on the work environment. In today's fast-paced economy, business and other professionals find themselves in situations that require quick actions, and these include making quick and wise decisions. While the decision-making process discussed earlier in this chapter is fundamental to learning effective decision-making skills, there comes a time when decision makers must rely more on quicker, yet reliable, methods.

The decision-making process and other traditional decision making models focus on problems and past events that caused problems. Current thinking about making decisions is beginning to focus more on possibilities and future desired outcomes. One model, created by Bostrom and associates, is called outcome-directed thinking. The research in this approach to decision making indicates that the use of outcome-directed thinking tends to illicit more creative ideas, more positive reactions and more optimism from those who use this approach. Bostrom and associates recommend the following steps in applying outcome-directed thinking:[9]

Step 1: Think of a problem you have in your life right now for which something is not what you would like it to be. It could be any problem you are having at school, home or work that you would like to solve. Write a few words below that summarize that problem:

Step 2: Briefly answer the following questions:

- What do I really want instead of this problem? (State your answer as your desired future outcome.)

- How will I know when I have achieved this future outcome?

- What resources do I need to pursue this future outcome?

- What is the first step I can take to achieve this outcome?

Step 3: Discuss your answers to the questions with at least one other person. Ask for feedback, and at the same time reflect on your thoughts with regard to creativity and usefulness of your proposed solution. Is your solution something that can be implemented? Is your proposed solution realistic? Do you have the resources with which to implement your ideas?

Decision-Making Pitfalls

Although working in groups and teams has many benefits, it is important to raise awareness of the potential pitfalls. There are five key areas for groups and teams to watch in order to avoid negative impacts on their progress. The five key areas include groupthink, escalation of commitment, the Abilene Paradox, group polarization and unethical decision making.[10]

Groupthink

Definition: Groupthink occurs when members of a group fail to express opinions that oppose those of other members of the group. Groupthink results from the desire of group members to maintain unity and harmony within the group members versus making the best decision possible.[11]

Example: A group/team is assigned to develop a new process for the production of a new product. As the group approaches the end of the project, a member of another department shares information with a member of the group that could potentially affect the group's progress. The group member does not place importance on the new information because of loyalty to the group, assuming that the group has to be right in their findings.

Symptoms: Some of the most common symptoms of groupthink include:

- Feeling invulnerable
- Believing the group has ultimate morality
- Feeling pressure to dissent
- Rationalizing with the group by being biased

Potential consequences of groupthink include:

- Failure to review all alternative solutions
- Biased choices
- Limited search of information
- Lack of alternative plans

Tips for teams: Avoid groupthink by following these suggestions:

- Limit group size; form subgroups, if necessary
- Share concerns privately by writing down comments anonymously
- Invite team members to role play opposing positions
- Appoint someone to be a devil's advocate

Escalation of Commitment

Definition: Escalation of commitment occurs when a team continues to invest resources on an effort in spite of feedback that the solution is not effective.

Example: The group receives feedback about the solution to a problem. The feedback indicates that the solution is not working. Instead of "pulling the plug" on the project, the group continues in efforts to fix the solution, while the negative feedback continues.

Symptoms: The primary symptoms of escalation of commitment include:

- Negative feedback
- Increased cost
- Additional needed resources

Potential consequences of escalation of commitment include:

* Wasted resources
* Lack of approval
* Failure
* Dismissal from employment

Tips for teams:

* Set limits early on
* Avoid tunnel vision
* Be realistic about costs and resources
* Invite outsider's feedback

The Abilene Paradox

Definition: Groupthink and escalation of commitment tend to be the result of individual behavior in groups/teams. The Abilene Paradox is about team behavior that occurs when all of the members attempt to avoid conflict and end up with a result that no one wanted. With the Abilene Paradox, team members make decisions they believe other members want.

Example: The Abilene Paradox is named after an actual event that occurred in Texas. A group of individuals take a trip to Abilene, in extreme heat, with no air-conditioning to a restaurant for dinner. Once there, each individual expresses their dissatisfaction with the entire trip, the meal and other circumstances. They find out that no one wanted to make the trip; yet, each individual agreed to go because they believed the other members of the group wanted to go.

Symptoms:

* A member of the group is perceived to be an expert of some type.
* Lack of confidence
* Pressure to conform
* Dysfunctional behavior within the group

Potential consequences of the Abilene Paradox include:

* Failure to achieve team goals
* Loss of time and other resources

- Resentment
- Dissention from group norms

Tips for teams:

- Confront issues in a team setting
- Vote privately on issues
- Establish a forum for controversial issues
- Failure is a possibility; take responsibility

Unethical Decision Making

Definition: Unethical decision making occurs when the pressure of group-think, escalation of commitment and other biases creates an environment in which groups make decisions contrary to the benefit of the group and the organization. Unethical decision making is typically the result of a series of events as opposed to a single event.

Example: After receiving negative feedback on a group's project or solution, the group tries to cover up or misuse information to deflect blame or gain an undeserved advantage.

Symptoms:

- Lack of accountability
- Lies and withholding of information
- Secret meetings and alliances
- Lack of progress

Potential consequences of unethical decision making include:

- Illegal activity
- Failure
- Dissention
- Whistle blowing

Tips for teams:

- Avoid and/or eliminate conflicts of interest
- Tell the truth
- Create an environment of integrity
- Communicate

In summary, decision making is a common yet complex undertaking that takes place on a daily basis. Personal and business decisions, individual and group decision all have potentially lasting consequences. Chapter 8 attempts to present some simple approaches to decision making in the context of working in groups and teams. The contents of this chapter are, by design, simplified into a practical format that can be used for simple problems, complex problems and every problem in between. The purpose of the chapter's content is to provide effective and practical tools for decision making in the fast-paced work environment.

Review Questions

1 Define and describe the decision-making process.
2 Review basic decision-making alternatives.
3 How can you determine the best decision-making alternative to use?
4 Define and describe some decision-making pitfalls.

Note: Answers to the review questions are located in the Appendix.

Notes

* Einstein, A. (2013). The Biography Channel Web site. Retrieved from http://www.biography.com/people/albert-einstein-9285408

1. Goodwin, C., & Griffith, D. B. (2009). *Supervisor's survival kit* (11th ed.). Columbus, OH: Pearson/Prentice Hall.

2. Vance, C. M., Groves, K. S., Pail, Y., & Kindler, H. (2007). Understanding and measuring linear-nonlinear thinking style for enhanced management education and professional practice. *Academy of Management Learning & Education, 6*(2), 167–185.

3. Daft, R. (2012). *Management* (10th ed.). Mason, OH: South-Western.

4. Daft, R.

5. Charney, C. (1995). The manager's tool kit. New York, NY: American Management Association.

6. Charney, C.

7. Charney, C.

8. Daft, R.

9. Bostrom, R. P., & Clawson, V. K. (1996). Research-driven facilitation training for computer-supported environments. *Group Decision and Negotiation, 5*, 7–29.

10. Thompson, L. L. (2004). *Making the team* (2nd ed.). Upper Saddle River, NJ: Pearson/Prentice Hall.

11. Janis, I. L. (1982). Groupthink: Psychological studies of policy decisions and fiascoes (2nd ed.). Boston, MA: Houghton Mifflin.

Time-Management Competency
The Tool Kit for Effectiveness and Efficiency

Your time is limited, so don't waste it living someone else's life. Don't be trapped by dogma—which is living with the results of other people's thinking. Don't let the noise of others' opinions drown out your own inner voice. And most important, have the courage to follow your heart and intuition. They somehow already know what you truly want to become. Everything else is secondary.

—**Steve Jobs***

Introduction

Time management was briefly discussed in Chapter 4, Team Competency, for the purpose of illustrating one of the factors that affect team productivity. In Chapter 9, time management gets thorough coverage as a topic that is universal, as it affects every moment of each day.

We live in an extremely busy world. Young, middle-aged and older individuals share the work environment and social environment like never before. Everyone is busier than ever, and is constantly adding more activities to an already busy calendar. Why is this paradox occurring? Why do we counterintuitively add more activities to each day when we know we cannot add more hours to the day? Of all the variables in a given day, project or assignment, time is the most constant; there are only 24 hours in each day. The solution seems simple enough in that the only alternative left is to manage the time we do have. In fact, a quick search on Google for "time-management tips" yields 254 million hits. The same search on Yahoo yields 320 million hits. There is certainly plenty of supply and demand for the topic.

Chapter 9 Competencies

The purpose of this chapter is to help you:
- Review time-management principles.
- Analyze time-management issues in daily activities.
- Analyze time-management techniques.
- Apply time-management techniques.
- Understand the relationship between time management and stress.
- Discuss technology and time management.

Figure 9.1

Time-Management Myths

The overwhelming amount of information available on time management is evidence of the fact that we struggle with how we view, utilize and think about time. How did this happen? Human beings learn in a variety of ways, and one of the most available methods of learning about time management is through vicarious learning. Vicarious learning is the type of learning that occurs through observing others.[1] Over time, generations of people have observed and learned from their predecessors about habits, practices and other positive and negative concepts of time management. Some of the time management habits and practices that are not helping individuals to be more efficient are now included as myths in a number of resources.

The University of Illinois at Urbana–Champaign includes a list of time-management myths on their counseling center's Web site. The Web site also includes suggestions and specific techniques for effective time management. The time-management myths include the following items[2]:

MYTH: External events control my life.
FACT: Learn about what you can and cannot control before you make choices. In other words, making better choices is at the root of the issue.
MYTH: Feeling pressured to meet everyone's expectations.
FACT: Take control of your own expectations before you consider the expectations of others.
MYTH: I should have no limits.
FACT: Everybody has limits; admit it.

Time-Management Principles

Sales coach Cheryl Clausen states her interpretation of time management by first stating that she hates the term *time management*. Clausen's believes it is not about managing time but rather about managing the way we use our time. While some time-management experts believe that time management is about tracking time by writing everything down in a calendar or planner, Clausen believes managing our time is about the following steps[3]:

- Setting clear objectives.
- Identifying what needs to occur to produce the objectives.
- Tracking successful actions and results.

- Being at the right place at the right time.
- Sticking to the plan while being prepared for the unexpected.

Kathy Peel is a family manager and coach who shares her thoughts about time management in her blog. Her list of time-management realities include the following suggestions[4]:

- No perfect planning system exists.
- While no system is perfect, no system at all is crazy.
- Plan; you can't predict.
- Know your personal priorities.
- Life is more about rhythm than balance.
- Know your own rhythm for your life.

Perhaps Dr. Donald E. Wetmore of the Productivity Institute says it best. He has conducted more than 2,000 seminars and workshops on the time-management myth during the past 30 years. He believes most of our stress is due to unrealistic expectations we set for ourselves in thinking we can do everything that needs to be done. Dr. Wetmore says, "It is instructive that when we go to the funeral home to pay our respects to a dear departed friend, the focus is always on what that person did in their lives, not what they did not do. We celebrate one another's achievements and do not bemoan what they did not do. Yet, in our own lives many task themselves over what they are not doing, what they have not accomplished." Clearly, our focus needs to shift to what we can do instead of what we did not do by directing our energy toward those accomplishments that are most valuable to each of us.[5]

The six most important things you need to know about time management:[6]

1 Time is a nonrenewable resource.
2 Time is either used effectively or wasted.
3 Multitasking is a myth.
4 Wasting time causes stress.
5 Practice saying no.

- Fear of offending
- Caught off guard
- Feel needed
- Lack of goals and objectives (others will determine these for you)
- Fear of letting down your boss or other team members

6 Balancing time between work and personal life is important to your health.

The six most common time wasters[7]:

1 Anything that does not contribute directly to your goals and objectives
2 Lack of concentration
3 Too many meetings
4 Interruptions

- Set a time limit
- Encourage stand-up meetings
- Set appointments
- Avoid unnecessary conversation
- Avoid those who continually take advantage
- If asked, "Got a minute?"... say no

5 Multitasking
6 Procrastination[8]

- Lack of self-discipline
- Convincing yourself that you work better under pressure
- Lack of deadlines
- Failure to monitor your progress
- Doings easy tasks first; postponing the difficult tasks
- Unrealistic time estimates
- Trying to do too much

Procrastination analysis[9]:

1 Describe a current goal on which you are procrastinating.
2 What will you gain in achieving this goal?
3 What will you lose if you do not achieve this goal?
4 How much time will it take for you to finish this goal?
5 Do you have the necessary knowledge, skills and abilities to finish this goal? If no, what exactly do you need?
6 Are you confident about your abilities? If no, what do you need to do to build your confidence?
7 Identify the smallest step you can take to get started, and do it.

Analyze Time-Management Issues in Daily Business Activities

We hear so much about our changing world, a world without borders, and so on, in business meetings, on the news and other media. In one word, globalization covers the wide array of challenges and benefits of the current business environment. Globalization refers to the relationships the United States has with other countries regarding trade, information, investments, culture and social and political issues.[10]

Culture is the element of globalization that encompasses how individuals orient themselves toward time. Behavioral research supports the premise that understanding and learning about cultural differences can help avoid costly mistakes in conducting global business interactions.[11] Awareness and learning about cultural differences is the first step in managing the differences in how time can be managed. Differences are not good or bad, they are just different.

The benefits of conducting business on a global level do not come without significant challenges. One of the differences between the United States and China, for example, is in our perceptions of time. Americans tend to be focused on the business transaction while the Chinese value building relationships before conducting business transactions. Also, the Chinese culture is about long-term commitments while the American culture focuses on short-term rewards. Americans tend to be more abrupt and to the point in business meetings. The Chinese style is much more guarded and indirect. Punctuality is another area where the two cultures differ. Americans tend to be more flexible about punctuality, and the Chinese consider being late a sign of disrespect.[12]

These examples of conducting business between the United States and China are indicators of time-management factors that could impact business relationships. Developing relationships, long-term commitments and punctuality require time-management skills that will support a successful outcome.

France is another country with which the United States conducts significant business transactions. Generally speaking, the French are a polychronic culture in their views on time management. Polychronic cultures view time as just a portion of the whole. They use time to accomplish multiple tasks that are related to one another. Polychronic cultures are apt in doing several things at the same time. The United States, on the other hand, is considered a monochromic culture. Americans view time as a tangible resource which has value and can be measured.[13] Therefore, time is a "use it or lose it" commodity. Monochronic cultures like to do just one thing at a time, they like order and value having an assigned and appropriate time and place for everything. Here is a list of descriptions for monochronic and polychronic types[14]:

Table 9.1

Monochronic Values	Polychronic Values
Tend to do one thing at a time	Do several things at the same time
Are not easily distracted	Are susceptible to distractions
Commit to work	Commit to relationships
Place importance on deadlines	Place less importance on deadlines
Stick to plans	Change plans often and easily
Value and respect privacy	Value connection
Relate punctuality to reputation	Relate punctuality to the relationship
Accept short-term relationships	Lean toward lifetime relationships

The value of knowing the characteristics listed above is twofold. It is as important to understand your personal time management values as it is to understand time-management values of those from other cultures with whom you might work in a group or team.

Exercise:

Review the characteristics of a monochronic type and the characteristics of a polychronic type in the following chart. Mark the items with which you identify the most. The results should give you an indication of your preferences. Use the same approach when working with individuals from other cultures or when working in other countries. This knowledge will help you become aware of the differences, and also prepare you for what you should learn about how others manage time.

Table 9.2

Monochronic Characteristics	Polychronic Characteristics
Tend to do one thing at a time	Do several things at the same time
Are not easily distracted	Are susceptible to distractions
Commit to work	Commit to relationships
Place importance on deadlines	Place less importance on deadlines
Stick to plans	Change plans often and easily
Value and respect privacy	Value connection
Relate punctuality to reputation	Relate punctuality to the relationship
Accept short-term relationships	Lean towards lifetime relationships

In summary, Western cultural values differ from non-Western cultural values. Time management, for example, has a significant difference in how it is valued by Western and non-Western cultures. In Western cultures, time is money while in non-Western cultures, time is life.[15] As global business and multicultural project teams become the norm in the work environment, awareness of cultural differences followed up with training and education programs is no longer an option for successful organizations.

Time-Management Techniques

Richard Walsh, in his book titled *Time Management*, believes it is important to analyze how we spend our time by analyzing our activities for one week. Many time-management experts suggest the same approach; yet, Walsh's approach is unique because it includes comparisons among an estimate of the time spent on an activity, the ideal amount of time an individual wants to spend on an activity and the actual time spent on the activity.[16]

Let's say you think you will spend 10 hours at work. Since there are 24 hours in each day, 10 hours divided by 24 hours yields around 42% of the day that you anticipate you will spend working. The ideal amount of time spent at work might be 8 hours, and 8 hours divided by 24 hours equals approximately 33% of the day ideally spent at work. The third entry is the actual amount of time you spent at work. Assume you actually worked 12 hours that day, and 12 hours divided by 24 hours will yield 50% of the day spent working.

Example

Table 9.3

Activity: What do you plan to do today?	How much time do you think it will take?	How much time do you think it should take?	How much time did it take?
Work	10 (42%)	8 (33%)	12 (50%)
Analysis: Need to make adjustments to reduce number of hours at work each day. How?			
Activity			
Exercise	1 (4%)	2 (8%)	.5 (2%)
Analysis: Want to increase time spent exercising to at least one hour per day. How?			
Activity			
Drive to/from work	2 (8%)	1 (4%)	3.5 (15%)
Analysis: Is this the only route I can take to work? Investigate.			

Exercise:

Use the following chart to document how you spend the hours of a given day.

Table 9.4

Activity: What do you plan to do today?	*How much time do you think it will take?*	*How much time do you think it should take?*	*How much time did it actually take?*
Analysis:			
Activity			
Analysis:			
Activity			
Analysis:			

The value of keeping a log as suggested gives you the data you need to analyze how you spend your time during a given day. This type of information is useful in making adjustments that lead to good time-management practices. Taking charge of your time and how you spend it leads to living a more balanced life, can improve productivity and reduce stress.

Time Management and Stress

Stress impacts a life well lived on so many levels. The American Institute of Stress reports that stress is America's number one health problem.[17] In January, 2012, the American Psychological Association (APA) published its yearly survey results on stress in America, indicating a "deepening concern about the connections between chronic disease and stress." The most current survey does indicate that Americans are beginning to recognize the link between stress and illness; yet, little is being done to correct the situation. The APA suggests that a lack of effective time management might be the most significant reason underlying the lack of positive change.[18]

The significant sources of stress reported in the APA's 2012 Report include[19]:

- Money (75%)
- Work (70%)

- The economy (67%)
- Relationships (58%)
- Family responsibilities (57%)
- Family health problems (53%)
- Personal health concerns (53%)
- Job stability (49%)
- Housing Costs (49%)
- Personal safety (32%)

Stress-management strategies, reported by APA, tend to be more of a sedentary nature than exercise. The activities of choice, according the survey include[20]:

- Listening to music (48%)
- Exercising or walking (47%)
- Spending time with family or friends (39 percent)
- Napping (34%)
- Focusing on the positive (62%)
- Managing time better (56%)
- Being flexible and willing to compromise (53%)
- Avoiding people or situations that are stressful (53%)
- Expressing feelings instead of bottling them up (51%)
- Saying no (50%)
- Adjusting expectations (41%)

The National Institutes of Health (NIH) recommends a stress assessment for everyone on a regular basis by assessing attitude, diet, physical activity, support systems and relaxation. Some individuals do well with self-monitoring programs. If individuals do not do well working on their own, the NIH recommends professionals such as licensed social workers, psychologists and psychiatrists. Additional resources are listed on their Web site, http://www.nlm.nih.gov/medlineplus/ency/article/002150.htm[21].

Technology and Time Management

Plenty of research exists on the effectiveness of technology when it comes to time management. The software industry has provided numerous tools for the consumer, and the trend continues to expand. Recently, a *Businessweek* article suggested that the "very digital tools we count on to be more productive can also drag down our efficiency when they're used too much." The *Businessweek* special report also includes information about the cost of time-management issues. Specifically, digital interruptions in the work environment reportedly take up to 25% of the average worker's day and cost $650 billion a year in lost productivity. Up to 44% of technology use is spent on instant messaging, e-mail and social networking.[22]

Conclusion

The time-management facts, checklists, suggestions and other items included in Chapter 9 are by no means all inclusive. As stated in the beginning of the chapter, a multitude of information is available from numerous sources related to time management. Basically, there are two outstanding principles that make time management useful to individuals, groups, teams and organizations. The first principle is about awareness. Raising our awareness about how we spend our time is the first step in maximizing the use of our time. The second principle is about solutions. Once we are aware of what we are doing with our time, nothing will happen unless there is deliberate and planned action designed to remove obstacles and replace them with solutions. Here are some examples of the obstacles and solutions associated with effective time management[23]:

The competency-based approach of seeking knowledge, skills and abilities that make for successful and effective groups and teams comes to conclusion in Chapter 10: Lifelong Learning. In Chapter 10, you will learn about the

Table 9.5

Time-Management Obstacles	Solutions: Effective Time Management
Unfinished tasks	Prioritize and make wise choices
Perfectionism	Nobody is perfect—let go of unnecessary details
Multitasking	Do one thing at a time, and do it well.
Failure to organize and plan	Define objectives and how to reach them.
Hoarding	Clean out the junk. If you have not used it for six months, you probably do not need it.

synchronicity of all the chapters in this book. Developing competencies is a continuous process, and lifelong learning is the "etc."

Review Questions

1   Review-time management principles by comparing Cheryl Clausen's and Kathy Peel's perspectives.

2   What did you learn about Dr. Wetmore's time-management myth?

3   Analyze time-management issues in daily activities by describing whether you agree or disagree with the six most important things you need to know about time management.

4   Describe the six most common time wasters, and discuss your view on how useful this list is in learning time-management techniques.

5   Do you share monochronic or polychronic time-management values? Why is this important while working with people from different cultures?

6   Briefly describe the relationship between time management and stress.

7   Discuss the pros and cons of a dependence on technology for time management.

Note: Answers to the review questions are located in the Appendix.

Notes

*   Jobs, S. (2005). Stanford University commencement speech. Retrieved from news.stanford.edu/news/2005/june15/jobs-061505.html

1.   Daft, R. (2012). *Management* (10th ed.). Mason, OH: South-Western.

2.   University of Illinois at Urbana-Champaign. (2007). *Myths about time management*. Retrieved from http://www.counselingcenter.illinois.edu/?page_id=123

3.   Clausen, C. A. (2009, March 3). *Time management—The myths and the facts*. Retrieved from http://ezinearticles.com/?Time-Management—The-Myths-and-the-Facts&id=2058760

4.   Peel, K. (2009, July 8). *Time management myths*. Retrieved from http://www.parentdish.com/2009/07/08/time-management-myths/

5.   Wetmore, D. E. *The time management myth*. Retrieved from www.balancetime.com

6.   Alexander, R., & Dobson, M. S. (2008). *Real-world time management*. AMACOM. Retrieved from Ebook Library.

7. Alexander & Dobson.
8. Alexander & Dobson.
9. Alexander & Dobson.
10. Dafi, R.
11. Wong-MingJi, D.J. (n.d.). *International cultural differences.* Retrieved from http://www.referenceforbusiness.com/management/Gr-Int/International-Cultural-Differences.html
12. Expertise in Labour Mobility. (2011, May 10). *3 main differences in management culture between the US and China.* Retrieved from http://www.labourmobility.com/three-differences-in-management-culture-between-the-us-and-china/
13. Rochefort, P. (n.d.). *Intercultural management: Working with the French.* Retrieved from http://www.understandfrance.org/France/Intercultural3.html
14. Time Management Success. (n.d.). *Are you monochronic or polychronic?* Retrieved from http://www.time-management-success.com/polychronic.html
15. Anbari, F. T., Khilkhanova, E. V., Romanova, M. V. & Umpleby, S. A. (n.d.). *Cross cultural differences and their implications for managing international projects.* Retrieved from http://www.gwu.edu/~umpleby/recent_papers/2003_cross_cultural_differences_managin_international_projects_anbari_khilkhanova_romanova_umpleby.htm
16. Walsh, R. (2008). *Time management: Proven techniques for making every minute count.* Adams Media. Retrieved from Ebook Library.
17. The American Institute of Stress. *Workplace stress.* Retrieved from http://www.stress.org/workplace-stress/
18. American Psychological Association. (2012, January 11). *Latest APA survey reveals deepening concerns about connection between chronic disease and stress.* Retrieved from http://www.apa.org/news/press/releases/2012/01/chronic-disease.aspx
19. American Psychological Association.
20. American Psychological Association.
21. National Institutes of Health. (n.d.). *Stress management.* Retrieved from http://www.nlm.nih.gov/medlineplus/ency/article/001942.htm
22. Ricadela, A. (2009, March 9). *High-tech time management tools.* Retrieved from http://www.businessweek.com/managing/content/mar2009/ca2009039_010841.htm

Lifelong Learning Competency
The Key to Future Success

A society's competitive advantage will come not from how well its schools teach the multiplication and periodic table, but from how well they stimulate imagination and creativity.

—Albert Einstein*

That is real freedom. That is being educated, and understanding how to think. The alternative is unconsciousness, the default setting, the rat race, the constant gnawing sense of having had, and lost, some infinite thing.

—David Foster Wallace**

Introduction

Chapter 10 is about sustaining the knowledge, skills and abilities learned over time. Sustainability, in a business context, means renewal; it is about using and maintaining resources. How do competencies, once developed, continue to evolve? How can competencies be sustained beyond formal education?

The primary emphasis of this book is on competencies, or the synergy of knowledge, skills and abilities needed for effective group work and teamwork. Chapter 10 contains theory and exercises to help individuals continue their development of the competencies necessary for effectiveness in individual, group and team activities as a lifelong journey.

Initially, the chapters in this book addressed those critical aspects of what an individual contributes to the world. Additional chapters delved into the individual's relationship with their immediate group or team. Information associated with the interactions of groups and teams outside their immediate environment followed. Finally, Chapter 10 essentially provides a perspective for the future.

Chapter 10 Competencies

The purpose of this chapter is to help you:
- Understand the concept of lifelong learning.
- Identify components of lifelong learning.
- Develop a lifelong learning plan.
- Discover resources useful for lifelong learning activities.

Figure 10.1

What Is Lifelong Learning?

First, read the following comments and answer yes or no if you take part in the activities at least once a week.[1]

Exercise

Table 10.1

Yes	No	Activity
		1 I enjoy reading.
		2 I keep a list of things I want to learn.
		3 I enjoy intellectual discussions.
		4 I enjoy journaling, reflecting and/or meditating.
		5 I practice what I learn.
		6 I like to teach others what I learn.
		7 I avoid hoarding information sources such as blogs, data and so on.
		8 I join groups in which I can further my learning.
		9 I avoid making assumptions about anything.
		10 I like to work where learning is encouraged.
		11 I start a project in order to learn more about the subject.
		12 I follow my intuition.
		13 I use the beginning of my day to learn something new.
		14 I learn things that I can put to use.
		15 I make learning a priority.
		16 Have fun.
		17 Find your rhythm.
		18 Travel.
		19 Socialization.
		20 Give back.

Review your answers to the list of items. The *yes* answers identify the activities in your daily routines that support lifelong learning. The *no* answers identify areas in which you might want to add some activities to your daily schedule to increase lifelong learning support.

Lifelong learning refers to the benefits of pursuing knowledge, skills and abilities throughout life, after and beyond formal education pursuits. The concept of lifelong learning is not new. Two intellectuals, Eduard Lindeman and Basil Yeaxlee, formally introduced lifelong learning concepts as early as 1926 and contributed to the recognition of lifelong learning as a viable pursuit.[2] Lindeman and Yeaxlee drew from the early concepts of adult education to highlight the need for lifelong learning. One of the key elements of their interest in nonconventional education is on the learner's opportunity to reflect on past experiences as part of new learning. Lifelong learning is unique in that its value increases with an individual's prior knowledge and experience.

The U.S. Department of Education, through the National Center for Education Statistics, conducted a study titled "Participation in Adult Education and Lifelong Learning: 2000–2001. One of the results of the study emphasized the difference between formal education and lifelong learning. Lifelong learning is linked to informal learning, where the learning is much less formal, less structured and one in which the control is primarily the learner's responsibility. The primary activities pursued by lifelong learners in work-related informal learning included mentoring, self-paced study using manuals, videos, online courses, informal presentations, conferences and/or reading professional journals. The survey also reported that only one in five adults participated in personal-interest types of learning. About 50% of the participants in the study took courses and instruction from a variety of sources, such as community centers, public libraries, private organizations and religious organizations. Twenty percent of the respondents learned from postsecondary institutions and 17% from industry or business sources.[3]

Experts in the field of lifelong learning suggest that embracing the practice is akin to developing a new habit. Individuals adjust to daily routines responsibilities and tend to focus on essential learning, and leaving any other type of learning as an option. As Marcel Proust once said, "The real voyage of discovery consists not in seeking new lands, but in seeing with new eyes." One study suggests 20 steps to cultivate lifelong learning, and an additional five steps have been added based on general information found in the literature.[4]

Twenty Steps to Cultivate Lifelong Learning

1 **Books:** Always have a book to read, a little at a time.
2 **Lists:** Keep a "to learn" list of things you have always wanted to learn.
3 **Think:** Get more intellectual friends; people who like to think and learn.

4 **Guided thinking:** Spend time journaling, meditating or reflecting on ideas.

5 **Practice:** Apply your knowledge by doing something with the information you have learned.

6 **Teach:** Communicate your ideas to others by teaching, starting a blog, mentoring someone or simply discussing ideas with a friend.

7 **Focus on what counts:** There is so much information available today that it is important to focus on what counts.

8 **Learn in groups:** Join organizations, take workshops and make learning a social experience.

9 **Unlearn assumptions:** Challenge your way of thinking by seeking out information that opposes your views.

10 **Find jobs that encourage learning:** Consider a job and career that encourages intellectual freedom.

11 **Start a project:** Set out to do something new, and learn from the experience.

12 **Follow your intuition:** Stretch your imagination by listening to your "gut feeling."

13 **The morning 15:** Use the first 15 minutes of the day to learn something.

14 **Reap the rewards:** Learn information that is useful in your daily activities.

15 **Make it a priority:** Give lifelong learning the importance you want it to have.

16 **Have fun:** Productivity and having fun are not mutually exclusive concepts.

17 **Find your rhythm:** Make it a point to spend time working as well as relaxing. Instead of trying to find a balance between working and relaxing, try finding your rhythm.

18 **Travel:** Discover new places and enrich your life with different perspectives.

19 **Socialize:** Spend time with others on a social level for no other reason than to catch up on each other's lives.

20 **Give back:** Volunteer, share and give back to others.

Components of Lifelong Learning

Lifelong learning activities occur on a daily basis. The challenge lies in taking advantage of these daily opportunities to maximize the impact on predetermined goals, such as effective teamwork. Each of the competencies described in this book's chapters are carefully selected to create the synergistic gains of working together toward a common goal.

The following is a review of each of the chapters, designed to create additional context between each competency and lifelong learning. Each chapter's goals are reviewed with 2 of the 20 steps for lifelong learning described previously.

Chapter 1: Building Relationships

The goals of Chapter 1 are:

- Identify and describe the human side of teamwork.
- Know and understand the role of interpersonal skills.
- Analyze the correlation between teamwork and other social relationships.

In the list of 20 steps to cultivate lifelong learning, the first two steps are about reading books and maintaining a "to learn" list. Chapter 1 is about building relationships by focusing on the human side of team work. What are some activities that could increase proficiency in identifying and describing the human side of teamwork? How can you further understand the role of interpersonal skills? Which social relationships do you need to develop to sustain your relationships with team members?

Suggestions for continued development of the relationships needed for successful teamwork based on reading books and maintaining a "to learn" list might include some of the activities you are currently pursuing. In the exercise area below, list specific tasks you currently undertake.

Exercise:

List current lifelong learning activities designed to promote continuous learning about building relationships. Identify the frequency of each activity as well.

Table 10.2

Activity	Frequency
Books:	
Books:	
"To learn list":	
"To learn list":	

Analyze your responses, and consider how satisfied you are with your entries. The benefit of conducting this quick exercise is primarily to help you determine your success in applying Steps 1 and 2 of your lifelong learning plan for the future.

Following are some suggestions of activities you might consider adding to your list of lifelong learning tasks that promote continuous learning about building relationships, based on Steps 1 and 2 of the lifelong learning steps.

Table 10.3

Activity	Frequency
Books: *Scores on the Board: The 5-Part System for Building Skills, Teams and Businesses* by B. Lang, 2012	Read 1 chapter per week
Books: *Teamwork is an Individual Skill: Getting Your Work Done When Sharing Responsibility* by M. A. Walker, C. M. Avery & E. O. Murphy	Read 1 chapter per week
"To learn list": Study my behavioral preferences; take the MBTI Assessment.	Within the next 6 months
"To learn list": Reflect on my experiences by starting and maintaining an ongoing journal.	Within the next 6 months

Remember, you can always add to your list or adjust it as you see fit.

Chapter 2: The Inner-Self Competency

The goals of Chapter 2 are:

- Apply concepts of self-development to the teamwork environment.
- Practice techniques suitable for learning through self-reflection.
- Review personality theory in the context of teamwork.
- Apply personality theory concepts to ongoing self-development practices.

The next two steps in developing lifelong learning practices are about thinking. Step 3 encourages the development of intellectual exchanges, while Step 4 recommends guided thinking. Chapter 2 discusses the importance of knowing yourself, your habits and preferences in dealing with others. Practice applying Steps 3 and 4 while considering the content of Chapter 2. What are some activities that could increase proficiency in identifying and describing yourself in terms of self-development? How can you further understand the role of interpersonal skills and self-development? Which personality attributes do you need to develop to sustain your relationships with team members?

Exercise:

List current lifelong learning activities designed to promote continuous learning about self-development. Identify the frequency of each activity as well.

Table 10.4

Activity	Frequency
Spend time with intellectuals:	
Spend time with intellectuals:	
Guided thinking:	
Guided thinking:	

Analyze your responses and consider how satisfied you are with your entries. The benefit of conducting this quick exercise is primarily to help you determine your success in applying Steps 3 and 4 of your lifelong learning plan for the future.

The next section contains some suggestions of activities you might consider adding to your list of lifelong learning tasks that promote continuous learning about self-development based on Steps 3 and 4 of the lifelong learning steps.

Table 10.5

Activity	Frequency
Spend time with intellectuals: Create a book club to discuss the books you read about team building, self-development and so on.	Within the next 6 months, and then monthly
Spend time with intellectuals: Create a discussion group at work to discuss the books you read over lunch.	Within the next 6 months, and then monthly
Guided thinking: Reflect on my experiences by maintaining the journal you started in the Chapter 1 discussion.	Daily
Guided thinking: Look into meditation to determine its fit for you.	Within the next 6 months

Practice in these areas will give you more ideas in the future.

Chapter 3: Diversity

The goals of Chapter 3 are:

- Describe seven types of stereotypes found in today's work environment.
- Apply available resources that can be used to promote inclusion.
- Explain the relationship between personality and diversity in the workplace.

Chapter 3 is about diversity and inclusion, and Steps 5 and 6 will serve as examples for this continuing discussion of lifelong learning. Step 5 calls for putting into practice what we learn as we develop lifelong learning skills. Step 6 recommends teaching others the new skills and practices as they are learned.

Exercise:

List current lifelong learning activities designed to promote continuous learning about diversity through practicing and teaching associated skills. Identify the frequency of each activity as well.

Table 10.6

Activity	Frequency
Practice:	
Practice:	
Teach:	
Teach:	

Analyze your responses, and consider how satisfied you are with your entries. The benefit of conducting this quick exercise is primarily to help you determine your success in applying Steps 5 and 6 of your lifelong learning plan for the future.

Following are some suggestions of activities you might consider adding to your list of lifelong learning tasks that promote continuous learning with regard to practicing and teaching skills about diversity based on Steps 5 and 6 of the lifelong learning steps.

Table 10.7

Activity	Frequency
Practice: Organize a get-together and invite people of diverse backgrounds.	Every 6 months
Practice: Learn a different language and practice with those who speak that language, perhaps over coffee or lunch.	Within the next year
Teach: Select a group from the inclusive diversity model found in Chapter 3, and mentor someone from that group.	Within the next 6 months
Teach: Select a group from the inclusive diversity model found in Chapter 3, and invite that person to watch a particular movie or program. Discuss the movie or program over coffee.	Within the next 6 months

There are many resources online with regard to diversity in Chapter 3.

Chapter 4: Team Competency

The goals of Chapter 4 are:

- Know the difference between groups and teams.
- Understand the 10 key challenges faced by group and team members.
- Describe the five steps of team development.
- Learn how to manage five team dysfunctions.

Groups, teams, team development and team dysfunctions are the topics discussed in Chapter 4. Steps 7 and 8 of the lifelong learning development list will serve as the context for Chapter 4. Step 7 describes the importance of maintaining data and other sources of information in order to focus on what is important and useful. Step 8 refers to the benefits of learning in groups.

Exercise:

List current lifelong learning activities designed to promote continuous learning about groups and teams. Identify the frequency of each activity as well.

Table 10.8

Activity	Frequency
Focus on what counts:	
Focus on what counts:	
Learn in groups:	
Learn in groups:	

Analyze your responses and consider how satisfied you are with your entries. The benefit of conducting this quick exercise is primarily to help you determine your success in applying Steps 7 and 8 of your lifelong learning plan for the future.

The next section contains some suggestions of activities you might consider adding to your list of lifelong learning tasks that promote continuous learning about groups and teams based on Steps 7 and 8 of the lifelong learning steps.

Table 10.9

Activity	Frequency
Focus on what counts: Purge e-mails from your account.	Every 3 months
Focus on what counts: Recycle magazines, brochures and other types of documents.	Every 3 months
Learn in groups: Attend a workshop sponsored by a community or city group.	Every 6 months
Learn in groups: Attend a business conference.	Once a year

Patience helps with these areas, and you do not have to do it all at once.

Chapter 5: Social Networks and Communicating Effectively in the Team Environment

The goals of Chapter 5 are:

- Reflect on what you already know about the communication process.
- Learn fundamental communication process and model principles.
- Apply communication principles to team communication practices.
- Assess social networking strategies in the context of the team environment.

Chapter 5 includes discussions on topics ranging from communication theory to social networking. Consider the contents of Chapter 5 to review

Steps 9 and 10 of the lifelong learning plan. Step 9 suggests that the learner should actively avoid having too many convictions which tend to lead to making assumptions. In Step 10, the learner is encouraged to seek out jobs and careers that encourage and support continual learning.

Exercise:

List current lifelong learning activities designed to promote continuous learning about communication. Identify the frequency of each activity as well.

Table 10.10

Activity	Frequency
Avoid assumptions:	
Avoid assumptions:	
Find jobs that encourage learning:	
Find jobs that encourage learning:	

Analyze your responses and consider how satisfied you are with your entries. The benefit of conducting this quick exercise is primarily to help you determine your success in applying Steps 9 and 10 of your lifelong learning plan for the future.

Following are some suggestions of activities you might consider adding to your list of lifelong learning tasks that promote continuous learning about communication based on Steps 9 and 10 of the lifelong learning steps.

Table 10.11

Activity	Frequency
Avoid assumptions: Find a TV, radio or online program you would not otherwise watch or listen to due to your beliefs. Watch the program, and reflect on the differences.	Once a month
Avoid assumptions: Listen to a politician from an opposing party, and think about the differences.	Every 6 months
Find jobs that encourage learning: Volunteer at a local nonprofit organization, such as Meals on Wheels or the public library.	Once a month
Find jobs that encourage learning: Volunteer to teach a class at a local community center or public library.	Once a month

Online searches for information in these areas are useful.

Chapter 6: Environment Competency

The goals of Chapter 6 are:

- Describe several types of organization structures found in today's work environment.
- Understand the relationship between organization structure and strategic goals.
- Explain the relationship between teamwork and organization structure in the workplace.
- Apply available resources that can be used to promote productivity in the team's environment.

Chapter 6 describes the structure and other surroundings of the workforce that are called the work environment. Of particular importance is the concept of an organization's strategic goals and how they impact the work of groups and teams. Steps 11 and 12 are the lifelong learning steps for discussion along with Chapter 6. Step 11 promotes starting projects as learning tools. The value of intuition is the subject of Step 12.

Exercise:

List current lifelong learning activities designed to promote continuous learning about the group and team environment. Identify the frequency of each activity as well.

Table 10.12

Activity	Frequency
Start a project:	
Start a project:	
Follow your intuition:	
Follow your intuition:	

Analyze your responses, and consider how satisfied you are with your entries. The benefit of conducting this quick exercise is primarily to help you determine your success in applying Steps 11 and 12 of your lifelong learning plan for the future.

The next section contains some suggestions of activities you might consider adding to your list of lifelong learning tasks that promote continuous learning about the group and team environment based on Steps 11 and 12 of the lifelong learning steps.

Table 10.13

Activity	Frequency
Start a project: As a project, learn about the field of project management.	Within 1 year
Start a project: Start a new project designed to help you remodel a room in your house or a friend's house.	Within 1 year
Follow your intuition: Practice making quick decisions on simple dilemmas, such as where to go for lunch.	Once a month.
Follow your intuition: Take a day trip to a new location without planning the event.	Once every 6 months

Basic project management skills can provide enormous guidance.

Chapter 7: Business Ethics & Social Responsibility Competency

The goals of Chapter 7 are:

- Review ethics principles and practices in business.
- Describe the relationship between ethics, the law and free choice.
- Understand the principles of social responsibility.
- Define sustainability and why it is important.
- Apply ethics principles to establishing an ethical environment.

The content of Chapter 7 presents concepts with regard to ethics and social responsibility in the work environment. Steps 13 and 14 serve as the examples of the Lifelong Learning steps for this chapter.

Exercise:

List current lifelong learning activities designed to promote continuous learning about ethics and social responsibility. Identify the frequency of each activity as well.

Table 10.14

Activity	Frequency
Beginning of the day:	
Beginning of the day:	
Reap the rewards:	
Reap the rewards:	

Analyze your responses and consider how satisfied you are with your entries. The benefit of conducting this quick exercise is primarily to help you determine your success in applying Steps 13 and 14 of your lifelong learning plan for the future.

Following are some suggestions of activities you might consider adding to your list of lifelong learning tasks that promote continuous learning about ethics and social responsibility based on Steps 13 and 14 of the lifelong learning steps.

Table 10.15

Activity	Frequency
Beginning of the day: Create a personal code of ethics, adding to the list each day. You do not have to finish it in one sitting.	Daily
Beginning of the day: Using the Internet, search and read different company's ethics statements and codes of ethics.	Once a week
Reap the rewards: Use the information you learn about ethics statements to help your group or team develop an ethics statement.	Within 1 year
Reap the rewards: Use the information you learn about codes of ethics to help your group or team develop a code of ethics.	Within 1 year

You might consider speaking with people who work for large corporations to gain more insight into ethics and social responsibility.

Chapter 8: Decision-Making Competency

The goals of Chapter 8 are:

- Analyze the decision-making process.
- Review basic decision-making alternatives.

- Determine the best decision-making alternative to use.
- Understand some decision-making pitfalls.

Chapter 8 focuses on the decision-making process. Making effective decisions, recognizing alternatives to decision making and some of the pitfalls involved is the context for reviewing Steps 15 and 16. Step 15 recommends making lifelong learning a priority because no one else is going to make that decision for you. In Step 16, the emphasis is on having fun.

Exercise:

List current lifelong learning activities designed to promote continuous learning about decision making. Identify the frequency of each activity as well.

Table 10.16

Activity	Frequency
Make it a priority:	
Make it a priority:	
Have fun:	
Have fun:	

Analyze your responses and consider how satisfied you are with your entries. The benefit of conducting this quick exercise is primarily to help you determine your success in applying Steps 15 and 16 of your lifelong learning plan for the future.

The next section contains some suggestions of activities you might consider adding to your list of lifelong learning tasks that promote continuous learning about decision making based on Steps 15 and 16 of the lifelong learning steps.

Table 10.17

Activity	Frequency
Make it a priority: Write and sign a contract about committing to a lifelong learning plan.	Within 1 year
Make it a priority: Discuss your lifelong learning plan with others to raise awareness about your commitment.	Within 1 year
Have fun: If you like comedy, make it a point to find and attend comedy stand-up clubs.	Once a month
Have fun: Find appropriate gadgets and "toys" to keep on your desk.	Within the next 6 months

Start with small, achievable steps.

Chapter 9: Time-Management Competency

The goals of Chapter 9 are:

- Review time-management principles.
- Analyze time-management issues in daily activities.
- Analyze time-management techniques.
- Apply time-management techniques.
- Understand the relationship between time management and stress.
- Discuss technology and time management.

Time management is the topic of Chapter 9, and Steps 17 and 18 are the lifelong learning steps for this section. Step 17 encourages finding a rhythm for your life, while Step 18 recommends travel.

Exercise:

List current lifelong learning activities designed to promote continuous learning about time management. Identify the frequency of each activity as well.

Table 10.18

Activity	Frequency
Find your rhythm:	
Find your rhythm:	
Travel:	
Travel:	

Analyze your responses and consider how satisfied you are with your entries. The benefit of conducting this quick exercise is primarily to help you determine your success in applying Steps 17 and 18 of your lifelong learning plan for the future.

Following are some suggestions of activities you might consider adding to your list of lifelong learning tasks that promote continuous learning about time management based on Steps 17 and 18 of the lifelong learning steps.

Table 10.19

Activity	Frequency
Find your rhythm: Schedule an hour of "down time" for yourself to do nothing but sit in a comfortable place and relax.	Once a week
Find your rhythm: Spend a few hours at a coffee shop or café and enjoy the scenery, watch people and have a cup of coffee or a drink of your choice.	Once a week
Travel: Take a tour of your own city to discover the highlights of your immediate surroundings.	Once a year
Travel: Find the places of interest in a 50-mile radius from your home, and take a road trip of discovery.	Once a year

You do not have to complete these tasks alone, take a friend or family with you.

Chapter 10: Lifelong Learning Competency

The goals of Chapter 10 are:

- Understand the concept of lifelong learning.
- Identify components of lifelong learning in daily activities.
- Develop a lifelong learning plan.
- Discover resources useful for lifelong learning activities.

Lifelong learning is the topic in Chapter 10. Use the last two steps of the lifelong learning plan to reflect on the application of these steps. Step 19 is about socialization, and Step 20 is about giving back.

Table 10.20

Activity	Frequency
Socialization:	
Socialization:	
Give back:	
Give back:	

Exercise:

List current lifelong learning activities designed to promote continuous learning about lifelong learning. Identify the frequency of each activity as well.

Analyze your responses and consider how satisfied you are with your entries. The benefit of conducting this quick exercise is primarily to help you determine your success in applying Steps 19 and 20 of your lifelong learning plan for the future.

The next section contains some suggestions of activities you might consider adding to your list of lifelong learning tasks that promote continuous learning about lifelong learning based on Steps 19 and 20 of the lifelong learning steps.

Table 10.21

Activity	Frequency
Socialization: Organize a get-together for a group or team of coworkers.	Twice a year
Socialization: Attend a sporting event with your coworkers, friends and/or family.	Once a year
Give back: Select a local nonprofit organization, and volunteer to help them for 2 hours.	Once a week
Give back: Mentor a young person who needs guidance.	Once a week

At this point, after completing the series of exercises, you should be ready to sit back and look at the lifelong learning plan as your next project. Putting ideas in writing helps to commit to them and increase the chances of success in any endeavor.

Review the 20 steps for cultivating lifelong learning. Remember that you do not need to do everything at once. Select one, two or three at a time or as many as you feel comfortable undertaking. The best approach to take is to have a plan and to use the steps outlined above as your goals. Once you begin, the key is to do what you said you were going to do. One important suggestion for starting the plan is to keep it simple. A basic plan includes the following steps:

1   Where are you now with regard to your future needs?
2   Where do you need to be in the future?
3   How do you get there?

This three-step planning process addresses the primary and most useful questions for immediate results. The first step translates into the needs analysis phase of planning. During the first step, it is important to review the 20 steps to cultivating lifelong learning habits to determine which ones need attention. The second step calls for setting learning objectives with regard to the steps in need of development. The third step is about the continuous feedback and evaluation needed to stay on track. The following is an example of how the process works.

Example: Select a Step in Need of Development

Table 10.22

Step to cultivating lifelong learning	Goals/Objectives	Evaluation
Books	Read a book about team building in the next month	Did not finish the book
Comments: Continue reading for an additional month		

Discover Resources Useful for Lifelong Learning Activities

A common thread in what we know about lifelong learning is that the learner is ultimately responsible for its success. One approach for those who decide to engage in a serious lifelong learning effort is to have many resources of applicable information. This list of resources can help launch a successful lifelong learning program:

- Public libraries
- Professional organizations
- Community centers
- Religious organizations
- College and university alumni associations
- College and university libraries
- Nonprofit organizations
- Government offices
- Internet resources
- Examples of Internet resources
  - http://thinkfinity.org/literacy
  - http://www.infed.org/lifelonglearning/b-life.htm
  - http://learning.blogs.nytimes.com/2012/01/23/lifelong-learning-times-ideas-and-resources-for-keeping-your-brain-sharp/

- http://www.missiontolearn.com/2009/06/lifelong-learner-free-resources/
- http://www.acenet.edu/Content/NavigationMenu/ProgramsServices/CLLL/ResourceCenter/index.htm
- http://www.dlib.org/dlib/september96/kie/09hoadley.html
- http://www.helpguide.org/life/creative_play_fun_games.htm
- http://oedb.org/library/beginning-online-learning/the-self-directed-student-toolbox-100-web-resources-for-lifelong-learners
- http://www.lifelonglearning.co.uk/
- http://www.triadworks.org/Literacy/index.cfm
- http://www.lonestar.edu/all-tomball.htm
- http://www.eric.ed.gov/ERICWebPortal/search/detailmini.jsp?_nfpb=true&_&ERICExtSearch_SearchValue_0=ED181857&ERICExtSearch_SearchType_0=no&accno=ED181857
- http://www.usa.gov/
- http://www.usalearning.gov/USALearning/index.htm
- http://www.dest.gov.au/sectors/higher_education/publications_resources/other_publications/lifelong_learning_an_annotated_bibliography.htm
- http://www.google.com/search?q=www.lifelonglearningaccount.us%2Fresources.php&rls=com.microsoft:en-us:IE-Address&ie=UTF-8&oe=UTF-8&sourceid=ie7&rlz=1I7SUNA_en
- http://www.guardian.co.uk/government-computing-network/2011/oct/03/bis-lifelong-learning-accounts
- http://usgovernmentbenefits.org/hd/index.php?t=lifelong+learning+institute
- http://www.usdaw.org.uk/adviceresources/resources/orderforms/lifelonglearningpublications.aspx
- http://www2.ed.gov/offices/OERI/PLLI/index.html

What other resources can you add to the list of resources? One more step to cultivating lifelong learning habits could include adding resources to your list on a regular basis.

Conclusion

Lifelong learning concepts may have evolved from adult education practices in the past. The reality is that the workforce is aging as the baby boomer population continues to work well past their 60th birthday. At the same time, those entering the workforce have equally important learning needs. A report by the Life Long Learning at Work and at Home (Taskforce of the Association for Psychological Science) states, "We do not have a comparably educated cohort that can replace the large numbers of well-educated and highly-trained baby boomers at work, so it is in our economic best interest as a country to help older workers stay employed."[5]

The world continues to become more technical and complex, and with these changes comes the need for learning. The rapid changes seen in every aspect of business and other work environments continue to increase the need for employees who know how to learn and think. In addition, more and more, it is the learner's responsibility to acquire these skills. Lifelong learning habits seem to provide a timely and effective vehicle for the needs at hand.

Review Question

1   Develop a personal lifelong learning plan.

Note: Answer to the review question is located in the Appendix.

Notes

*   Einstein, A. (2013). The Biography Channel Web site. Retrieved from http://www.biography.com/people/albert-einstein-9285408

**   Wallace, D. F. (2009). *This is water: Some thoughts, delivered on a significant occasion, about living a compassionate life.* New York: Little, Brown and Company.

1.   Young, S. H. (2011, April 21). *15 steps to cultivate lifelong learning* [Web log post]. Retrieved from http://www.scotthyoung.com/blog/tag/lifelong-learning/

2.   Smith, M. K. (1996, 2001). *Lifelong learning: The encyclopedia of informal education.* Retrieved from http://www.infed.org/lifelonglearning/b-life.htm

3.   U.S. Department of Education. (2004, September). *National Center for Education Statistics. Participation in adult education and lifelong learning: 2000–2001.* Retrieved from http://nces.ed.gov/pubs2004/2004050.pdf

4.   Young, S. H.

5.   Association for Psychological Science. (2007, January). *Life long learning at work and home.* Retrieved from http://www.psychologicalscience.org/

Appendix: Chapter 1 Answers to Review Questions

1   Compare and contrast the human side of teamwork and the business side of teamwork.

A simple yet powerful and fundamental approach to building relationships in all aspects of life is to separate each interpersonal experience into two distinct and parallel dimensions. Every interpersonal transaction has two distinct dimensions or components: a human component and a business component. The degree of success in achieving the business component of an interaction is directly related to how the human portion of the exchange is approached. Studies suggest that the success of achieving a business goal improves when an individual approaches the event on the human side or with well-developed interpersonal skills.

While group members are skilled in the delivery of products and/or services, the missing link is often the development of relationships between the members of the group or team. Relationships are built through learning, developing and practicing interpersonal skills. Unfortunately, business-school curriculums tend to emphasize quantitative and qualitative skills much more than they do interpersonal skills. Failure to learn and develop interpersonal skills is a missed opportunity. The following scenario and exercises provide an introduction to the type of self-development activities that can lead to effective and efficient group work. The fundamental concept lies in our ability to learn. When people learn, they make changes in what they know and how they behave. Practice and experience are the primary drivers of learning.

2   Define interpersonal skills and why these are important skills in group and team environments.

While group members are skilled in the delivery of products and/or services, the missing link is often the development of relationships between the members of the group or team. Relationships are built through learning, developing and practicing interpersonal skills. Unfortunately, business-school curriculums tend to emphasize quantitative and qualitative skills much more than they do interpersonal skills. Failure to learn and develop interpersonal skills is a missed opportunity.

The fundamental concept lies in our ability to learn. When people learn, they make changes in what they know and how they behave. Practice and experience are the primary drivers of learning.

The reality lies in the failure to acknowledge and address behavioral issues in the workplace. Studies support the theory that the return on investment of group and team work is not realized when there is a lack of balance between technical, professional and interpersonal skills. After all, we are not computers and, even then, computers are not infallible.

3   Analyze the correlation between teamwork and other social relationships.

Developing interpersonal skills does not have to be a painstaking undertaking. Some potential group/team members might view the development of interpersonal skills as too "touchy-feely" and a waste of time. These types of interpersonal exercises might even remind some participants of group therapy that requires emotional openness. Some individuals prefer to spend valuable time addressing the task or deliverable that needs to be produced. The purpose of highlighting the value of learning interpersonal skills is to raise awareness in view of the validated success reported in research, studies and surveys of numerous corporate employees. Employees are not therapists nor are they psychologists, and that type of work should be left to the experts. Interpersonal skills are, nevertheless, another tool that can be used to leverage business success. Abraham Maslow's research supports this notion with his quote, "If all you have is a hammer, then everything looks like a nail" (14).

Appendix: Chapter 2 Answers to Review Questions

1   Discuss the importance of self-development as it relates to teamwork.

Who are you? First, the question must be placed in the proper context. Individuals have varying levels of knowledge, skills and abilities. Each learning experience has a cumulative effect on the competencies needed for effective group or team engagement. It is important to realize that the individuals who participate in a group/team might be at different readiness levels than those needed to achieve a common goal. The expectations set by the need to create the group do not always meet the group's ability to perform as a team. The first step for raising individual competency levels is to explore the area of self-awareness.

There are many ways in which a person can learn about him- or herself. Some of the most effective ways include self-reflection, feedback from others, open mindedness, and self-awareness. Learning activities include everything from formal educational experiences to self-development activities. Most formal educational experiences are structured and instructor led, while self-development activities are informal and self-directed. An individual can achieve maximum results from combining both types of learning.

Learning is something everyone does on a daily basis. Some individuals seem to absorb new information more readily than others, and the reasons for this are the subject of years of research. One study reports that only 14% of learning occurs in the classroom during a given year, and suggests that 53% of an individual's time is spent in community and home activities. The remaining 33% of the time is spent sleeping. The patterns observed in this study certainly support the notion that much of our learning experiences occur outside of the formal classroom.

2   Discuss useful techniques for learning through self-reflection.

During a panel discussion held at the Kellogg School of Management of Northwestern University, Clinical Professor Harry Kraemer defined self-reflection as "the process of silencing the noise and identifying goals." Visually, self-reflection is like picking up a camera, pointing it at yourself and taking a picture; a self-portrait. The key to effective self-reflection is the thought process that occurs after taking the self-portrait. It is about taking a past experience, thinking about it, assessing the pros and cons, and making a choice about how to approach future experiences.

Self-reflection can be overwhelming if more than one question is considered in one session. Simplification is important and can be achieved by taking one question at a time. The purpose of self-reflection is to achieve quality results, one step at a time; to do one thing well is usually more beneficial than to do many things badly.

Some individuals can go through a self-reflection exercise without hesitation, while others will struggle and find the process difficult. Whether you complete exercises like those in this book easily or not depends on several factors: style, experience, education, exposure and so on. Exposure to self-development activities can occur at home, at work, at school, at church or at a social event, to name a few of the possibilities. Self-assessment tests are bountiful and can be quite useful. Individuals involved with large organizations (schools and employers) usually have easy access to such tools as self-assessments. Together with training and education, self-assessments can provide valuable insight into an individual's knowledge, skills and abilities. In his *Self-Assessment Library,* Robbins states, "The *Self-Assessment Library* has been created to help you to learn more about yourself so that you might become 'enlightened'. It draws on numerous instruments that have been developed by behavioral researchers that tap into your skills, abilities, and interests". Theory and practice in the field of self-development asserts that the value of these activities is strongly correlated to successful interactions with others. Successful interactions with others are strongly correlated to improved performance.

Hellriegel and Slocum describe self-knowledge in terms of a competency; a self-competency. They define a self-competency as the "knowledge, skills, and abilities to assess personal strengths and weaknesses, set and pursue professional and personal goals, balance work and personal life, and engage in new learning." Self-knowledge, self-awareness and self-competency are only a few ways of describing the opportunity of knowing oneself better in a systematic way; as tools for improved business relationships. The theory and practice of developing self-knowledge might seem common sense to some, nevertheless it is a lost opportunity to many. Behavioral research consistently supports the positive relationship between individual competencies and behavior in general. These relationships are at the core of what happens when people work in groups or teams. Self-knowledge is critical because of the relationships between the individual, family/friends, work/society and the world. Self-development that occurs in tandem with these other entities tends to spill over into developing other competencies as well. The common factor that weaves throughout the relationships described previously is behavior, and behavioral researchers tie personality and behavior to characteristics that support productivity in teams.

3   What role does an individual's personality play in the team environment?

Personality is the one word that describes what makes an individual unique. An individual's personality also describes what a person has in common with others as well as what makes that person different. Behavioral researchers tend to agree that personality, while the result of many contributing variables, is usually affected the most by two primary influences. About half of personality traits are inherited from the genetic makeup of family characteristics. The other half of personality traits are developed through life experiences.

Organizations are well known for using personality tests to assess an employee's personality traits and attitudes during the hiring process, promotions and when assigning individuals to teams and work groups. Two of the most frequently used instruments are the *Minnesota Multiphasic Personality Inventory* (MMPI) and the *Myers-Briggs Type Indicator* (MBTI). These assessments identify behaviors which help employers determine relationships between personality and competencies in the work environment. Another important contributor to the study of individual characteristics is psychologist Daniel Goleman; he introduced the concept of emotional intelligence (EI). In spite of criticisms about the reliability and validity of Goleman's research, organizations are increasingly paying attention to EI because of the correlations between Goleman's research and career success. More specifically, EI refers to an individual's ability to handle interpersonal relationships. The areas of interest included in EI include self-awareness, social empathy, self-motivation and social skills. While technical skills can be determined by a variety of assessments, determination of interpersonal skills remains a challenge.

4   Discuss the role of personality theory concepts in ongoing self-development practices.

Study and analyze your traits, characteristics, and preferences because these individual attributes become contributing factors to the success or failure of an individual and of a team/group. Successful group work depends on factors such as balanced skill sets, a common purpose, specific goals, accountability and reliability. On the other end of the continuum of success, many groups/ teams fail to achieve their goals because of infighting, lack of trust, and lack of necessary skills. The common element in each of the outcomes is the ability of an individual to know, understand and develop individual interpersonal skills or competencies. Isabel Briggs Myers, one of the researchers who created the MBTI said it best: "When people differ, a knowledge of type lessens friction and eases strain. In addition, it reveals *the value of differences.* No one has to be good at everything. By developing individual strengths, guarding against known weaknesses, and appreciating the strengths of the other types, life will be more amusing, more interesting, and more of a daily adventure than it could possibly be if everyone were alike."

The individual's attitude is an additional important concept in the discussion of interpersonal skill development. Attitudes are the visible expressions, the evidence, of an individual's thoughts, feelings and behaviors.

A study about the effectiveness of work groups and teams by Kozlowski and Llgen clearly supports the value of pursuing proficient levels of interpersonal skills. The study's findings elaborate on the western world's focus on individual development while most work environments depend on the work of teams and groups. While schools educate individuals and corporations employ individuals, these same individuals are then assigned to teams with high expectations for their success. At the same time, little is formally done to enhance team training, development and leadership. Many research studies exist that provide processes which help individuals to combine their knowledge, skills and abilities with others to produce successful teams.

While there is evidence that individual competencies can influence team effectiveness, and that these competencies can be learned, the current educational structure must catch up with the needs of our organizations and institutions. Hence, the value of self-development becomes increasingly important.

Appendix: Chapter 3 Answers to Review Questions

Answers: Exercise—Diversity Exercise

Race/Ethnic Group

Franklin D. Raines—First African American to head a Fortune 500 Company

Sonia Sotomayor—First Hispanic U.S. Supreme Court Justice

Age/Stage of Development

John F. Kennedy—Youngest elected U.S. President

Ronald Reagan—Oldest elected U.S. President

Gender/Sexual Characteristics

Angela Merkel—Germany's first female leader

Six—Percentage of male Registered Nurses in the U.S.

Physical Ability/Bodily Strength

Stevie Wonder—World-famous blind pianist and singer

Erin Popovich—Best female athlete with a disability

Sexual Orientation/GLBT

1993–2011—Span of gays in the U.S. Military, "Don't Ask, Don't Tell"

Rachel Maddow—News anchor, political commentator, TV host, PhD and first openly gay American to receive a Rhodes Scholarship

Military Experience/Spent time in the military service

Vernice Armour—First African American female Combat Pilot

Frederick W. Smith—Went from being a Marine to chairman and CEO of FedEx

Personality/Set of individual characteristics

Albert Einstein—Mathematician/physicist with a learning disability

Mike Wallace—American journalist who suffers from clinical depression

Answers: Review Questions

1   Describe seven types of stereotypes found in today's work environment.

   a   Race/Ethnicity

   b   Age/Stage of Development

   c   Gender/Sexual Characteristics

   d   Physical Ability/Bodily Strength

   e   Sexual Orientation/ GLBT

   f   Military Experience/Spent time in the Military Service

   g   Personality/Set of individual characteristics

2   Why is it important to learn about diversity in the workplace?

Some of the most compelling reasons for including members of diverse groups in work teams include:

- Additional talent in the work environment
- Creative approaches to problem solving
- Improved decision making
- Competitive advantage due to a larger pool of talent

3   Regarding each type of stereotype described in Chapter 3, select one of the suggested resources and research the resource online. What new information did you find?

Answers will vary depending on the Web sites visited.

4   Explain the relationship between personality and diversity in the workplace.

The world of work is so diverse, that even an individual's personality is now considered a dimension of diversity. Personality is generally defined as the set of characteristics included in patterns of behavior used to respond to ideas, objects, or people in our daily environment. The result of years of research fits the findings about personality into the Big Five personality factors described in Chapter 2 (extroversion, agreeableness, conscientiousness, emotional stability and openness to experience). One additional trait that is included recently in the score of personality research is likability. Likeability is a subset of the agreeableness trait that includes friendliness, cooperation, understanding of others and helping others with positive self-worth.

Personality plays several important roles in how individuals work with others in groups and teams. Attitudes and behaviors are among the most important work-related attributes influenced by an individual's personality.

Appendix: Chapter 4 Answers
to Review Questions

1   Describe the main difference between groups and teams.

The most important aspect of groups and teams is that they all come together to accomplish a common goal. The primary difference between groups and teams lies in the process of how the work is managed to achieve a common goal. Groups usually consist of much more structure than teams. For example, groups tend to follow the structure of the organization that they represent. Groups tend to have designated roles, individual accountability and individual work products. Teams usually do not adhere to traditional organizational structure. Team members often collaborate on products by sharing both the work and the accountability for a job well done.

2   List and explain the 10 key challenges faced by group and team members.

a   Communication—Business communication is of utmost importance because the failure to communicate effectively can lead to significant consequences. Jobs are jeopardized, time is wasted, money is lost and relationships are adversely impacted when business communication fails to achieve a purpose.

b   Trust—Trust is based on many and varied characteristics; both personal and environmental characteristics and circumstances. Studies indicate that "The most fundamental determinants of trust however, are openness, honesty consistency, and respect." The most difficult aspect of trust development is that it is a give and take proposition. Someone has to take the first step in developing trust, and that is likely the most difficult step. An individual must be prepared to share information openly, reveal feelings, and take a risk. Building trust is an individual choice.

c   Conflict—Conflict is to be expected in building relationships with others, and building relationships is the cornerstone of teamwork. A misconception about conflict is that it can be resolved. Therefore, the goal in addressing conflict is to think in terms of managing not resolving the conflict.

Research indicates that a certain amount of conflict is actually beneficial in terms of creativity and productivity. Therefore, the issue is not the conflict itself. The issue is how individuals behave during a conflict. A conflict that results in cooperation and increased productivity is called positive or constructive conflict. The opposite is negative or destructive behavior which usually leads to lack of respect, decreases in productive and even bullying. Positive and negative behaviors in conflict management depend on an individual's personality, past experiences and a number of other traits and characteristics.

d   Commitment—Commitment is another foundation for effective team work. A commitment can be anything from a legally binding contract to a personal promise. When an individual commits to something, it means that energy, knowledge, skill and ability are dedicated to a successful outcome.

e   Accountability—Businesses around the world use the term accountability for strategy and planning to insure that business employees, processes and products are designed and managed to achieve a return on investment for the organization. In the context of working well with others, accountability has the same meaning. Accountability is the measurement of the contributions of each participant in achieving common goals.

Accountability is associated with fairness, honesty, and responsibility, both to oneself and to others. When individuals are accountable, they do what they say they are going to do. This promise of accountability can be supported by establishing performance management principles such as those found in organizations where productivity is measured against strategic, tactical, functional and individual goals. However, the path which leads to fulfillment of higher level goals depends on the input of individuals. In a group or team, individuals can provide valuable knowledge, skills and abilities, one person at a time.

f   Focus/caring—In a work environment, to care means to show concern and empathy for others. It does not mean that you have to take them home; just find a way to focus on the group's objective.

g   Time management—Time management is about using time wisely by choice. Good planning can improve choices, assuming there are no extenuating circumstances. Nevertheless, planning is a good habit to practice because it reduces wasting energy on unproductive activities. One aspect of time that is often overlooked is that there are only 24 hours in a day, and absolutely nothing can add even a second to that day.

h   Morale—A survey conducted by a management professor from Wichita State University revealed five characteristics in the work environment that support high morale. The five characteristics include: personal appreciation from a manager, written appreciation from a manager, performance-based promotions, public acknowledgement and meetings that build morale.

i   Common goals—Goals are the stepping stones that lead groups/ teams to success. Goals help set expectations, and expectations help identify individual contributions necessary for accomplishing a common goal. Setting realistic and achievable goals is a skill that can be learned and practiced with frequent use. Basically, goals should be specific and measurable. They should clearly state what needs to be done, the time allowed for completion of the tasks and a way to determine (measure) the results. The difficulty of a goal should be somewhere between too easy and too difficult; in other words, challenging. It is also very important that everyone in the work group participates in goal setting. This increases inclusion and accountability. Also, be sure to include a progress monitoring component in goals. Assess the progress made in achieving goals by providing continuous and mutual feedback.

j   Respect—Thinking about respect is useful to determine an individual's perspective regarding respect. Doirean Wilson of Middlesex University Business School in the United Kingdom writes about a review of the literature in "What Price, Respect." She summarizes the definitions of respect to include behavior that is considerate of others' feelings. Implicit in these definitions are moral values and dignity.

Working in groups and teams inevitably partners individual with others from different cultures, upbringings, religions and numerous other characteristics. Treating others with respect can be as simple as using the same techniques and approaches that one would want from others. This is not always an easy task; yet, the alternative usually results in negativity, anger, dysfunction and loss of productivity.

3   Describe the five steps of team development.

Forming—Group and team members get to know each other.

Storming—Group and team members begin to discuss, argue and position themselves.

Norming—Group and team members establish expectations and consequences for behavior.

Performing—Group and team members reach maturity and focus on productivity.

Adjourning—Group and team members finish their task and end their association.

4   List the five team dysfunctions and describe one managing tip for each of the dysfunctions.

Groupthink
- Encourage and maintain open communication.
- Assign a team member the role of "gate keeper" to observe for signs of groupthink.
- Stay focused on team and organizational goals.

Free riders
- Build accountability standards into the team goals and objectives.
- Conduct regular performance evaluations.
- Insist on open communication.
- Early on during team formation, make sure the team members have the set of skills, knowledge and abilities needed for team success.

Conflict
- Invest time during the initial meetings of your group or team. The time you invest up front will make the group or team experience much more productive, pleasant and fun.

- Establish ground rules for team activities and interactions.
- Insist on open communication.
- Address issues early on; do not let issues lie dormant.

Meetings
- Determine the reason for meeting.
- Make sure the right people are invited to attend.
- Plan the content and format of the meeting.

Difficult people
- Refer to the ground rules.
- Say that time is running out.
- Say that you must move on.
- Privately talk to the individual about time issues.
- Create smaller groups if possible.
- Create an agenda of additional concerns for a future meeting.

Appendix: Chapter 5 Answers
to Review Questions

1   Write a message intended for a team member. In the message, use the communication process to structure the content as clearly as possible.

Figure 5.2 The Communication Process

2   Describe the effects of noise on communication attempts based on the communication model.

Elements of the Communication Model

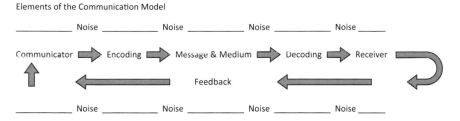

Figure 5.3 Elements of the Communication Model

Noise includes all of the environmental factors that can distort the message at every stage of the communication model/process. Noise includes time constraints, language barriers, misinterpretations and all of the examples included at each stage of the communication process.

The communication process and the communication model serve to set the foundation for all types of communication. These concepts are of particular importance in conducting business between individuals and among groups/ teams. One-on-one communication, although potentially complicated, tends to be easier to analyze in terms of its effectiveness. Since one-on-one communication is between two individuals, the potential for distractions and misinterpretations is limited compared to communication with more than one person. For example, in groups and teams, communication needs to occur between all of the members of the group. The number of individuals involved alone tends to introduce more noise into the conversations whether it is verbal, nonverbal, written and so on.

3   Why is it important to analyze the relationship between communication channels and number of team members?

Project management professionals attribute success in managing teams to a formula that helps them determine the complexity of communication in all teamwork. The premise for the formula is based on years of research and experience that has led them to assert that the ultimate success or failure of teamwork is dependent on one factor: communication. The formula these project managers use for determining effective communication among the team is $N(N - 1)/2$; where N is equal to the number of team members involved in a given project. The formula gives the communicator a number that equals the number of communication channels needed in order to make certain that each team member received the intended information. A communication channel is the path through which information passes between two individuals.

In a group or team of two participants, $N = 2$, and $2(2-1)/2 = 1$. The result of working the equation, the number one, indicates that effective communication should be disseminated through at least one channel between the two team members. In a group of three participants, effective communication calls for $3(3-1)/2 = 3$, or three channels of communication. In one more example, a group of 4 calls for $4(4-1)/2$, or six channels of communication. Clearly, the impact of adding one more person to a group of three increases the channels of communication significantly or twice as many channels.

4   Describe communication richness and how it relates to teamwork.

Communication in the business environment, between individuals, groups, teams, management, customers and other individuals is conducted in a variety of ways. The communicator is in charge of selecting the media of sending a message by considering the richness of the selected method. Richness of communication refers to the likelihood of creating mutual understanding about a topic. In other words, how can an individual create a mutual understanding among others in the most efficient and effective way?

A medium that provides the most richness with the most realistic immediate feedback is face-to-face communication. Face-to-face communication is best used for important messages that are best relayed in person. Yet, face-to-face communication is at times impractical and impossible when you consider distances and time. Telephone and video communications are considered rich media, especially when face-to-face communication is not possible or perhaps expensive (travel). Telephone and video channels of communication offer ways to communicate efficiently with immediate feedback. In today's environment, texting is included in this category of high richness. A lower level of richness in communication media includes memos, letters, faxes and voice mail. Although these are not as effective as face to face, telephone and video, they offer options that keeps information flowing. Lower richness media provides an efficient venue for cost-effective ways to communicate routine information, announcements and other general messages that need to be distributed to a large audience. The lowest richness for communication purposes is that of wide distribution e-mails, bulletin boards, flyers, financial reports and other types of reports. These methods are best used for wide distribution of standardized information.

5   Assess social networking strategies in the context of the team environment.

Communication and collaboration between team members has improved in recent years, with the use of other technologies. Project management professionals use blogs and wikis to communicate with team members and other project stakeholders in real time. In one study, the researchers found the importance in balancing the amount of communication in teams is the most important factor with regard to innovation and productivity. Too much communication tends to lead to groupthink, while too little communication leads to isolation.

The use of new and emerging technologies continues to improve efficiencies in communication that in turn enhance productivity for business groups and teams.

6   Conduct online research to find five current social networking sites. Are you currently using any of these sites for personal use? Describe the pros and cons of using these sites.

7   Conduct online research to find five current business networking sites. Which sites are you currently using? Describe the pros and cons of using these sites.

Appendix: Chapter 6 Answers
to Review Questions

1   Define the term *organization* and describe five functions served by an
    organization.

An organization by definition is a social entity with goals, direction, coordinated systems and structures, all linked to the external environment. Whether for profit or nonprofit, organizations serve the following functions:

- Coordinate resources for the achievement of organizational goals.
- Promote efficiencies in the production of products and services.
- Host innovations and creativity.
- Apply state of the art manufacturing and information technology.
- Navigate and influence the volatile environment.
- Provide value to all its stakeholders.
- Integrate the ongoing challenges presented by diversity, ethical dilemmas and the varied motivations of employees.

2   Name and describe the two primary dimensions of an organization.

Organizations consist of two dimensions: structural dimensions and contextual dimensions. These dimensions set the stage for how the organization maintains order while accomplishing goals. Structural dimensions include descriptions of the internal characteristics of the organization. Whether an organization is formal, specialized or centralized, the level of professionalism, personnel ratios and the chain of command are all included as characteristics of the structural dimension of an organization.

In formal organizations, documents exist that define and describe procedures, job descriptions, rules and policies. Formal institutions include large universities and corporations, such as those that deal in financial services. Small, family-owned businesses, on the other hand, tend to be more informal, with few written policies and procedures. Specialization within an organization is about whether employees focus on specific tasks or on general duties. Centralization refers to the decision-making level of the organization. When upper management reserves the decision making to their level of management only, the organization is described as centralized; when decision making drops to lower levels, it is said to be decentralized. Depending on the nature of the decision, some organizations can have centralized and decentralized decision-making roles throughout the levels of management and other employees. Professionalism in organizations is determined by the level of education and training among all employees. The personnel rations element of an organization's structural dimension describes the proportion of employees that work in the different departments.

The contextual dimensions of an organization include the characteristics that describe the entire organization. Contextual characteristics include the organization's size, technology, culture, environment, goals and strategy. The size of an organization is usually determined by the number of employees. Technology refers to the way in which the members of the organization perform their jobs. The culture consists of the unique practices and internal environment that define how work is performed in a particular organization. Environment refers to everything that exists outside the organization's boundaries. Finally, the goals and strategy are the part of the contextual dimensions that make the organization different from other organizations regarding its purpose.

3   What are the three environments and their components that affect an organization's activities?

Overview of the Task Environment:

- Customers—those who use and/or depend on the organization's goods or services.
- Competitors—those organizations, in the same business, that sell goods or services to the same customers.
- Suppliers—those who provide raw materials for the organization's use in producing goods or providing services.
- Labor market—the people in the organization's environment that can be hired to do work for the organization.

Overview of the General Environment:

- Technology—includes scientific and technological advances that impact how the organization operates.
- Natural environment—includes all aspects of the environment that are natural, such as plants, animals, natural resources and so on.
- Sociocultural—includes the values, customs of the general population in the general environment.
- Economics—includes purchasing power, unemployment rate, interest rates and other aspects of the economy that surrounds the organization.
- Legal/political—includes local, state and federal regulations along with political activities that influence the organization's operations.
- International—includes events from other countries that affect the organization.

Overview of the Internal Environment:

- Employees—those who work for an organization.
- Culture—the set of patterns of behavior and shared values about how things are done in the organization.
- Management—those who run the organization.

4 Why is an organization's structure important?

Organizations vary in structure, goals and purpose. They also range in size from multinational corporations to family-owned small businesses. Despite the many variations among organizations, they all have one thing in common: the people who work for the organization. In addition, organizations depend on the relationships their employees have with one another to help achieve organizational goals. Recent trends in management exist to improve relationships among employees by removing obstacles that in the past made collaboration and decision making complicated and time-consuming. One of the most successful changes in structuring and organizing work is in the increased dependence on groups and teams from different departments or areas within the organization to work together on assignments. This flattening of organizations is designed to improve horizontal communication between employees to successfully and consistently respond to our changing world.

The importance of organization structure is driven by the needs, goals and strategies of each department, function or process within the organization. The design of each organization is based on four primary factors: how the employees need to be grouped, based on their specialization or expertise; where employees need to work to best streamline their work and products; how management can best plan, organize, lead and control the work; and where the decision making needs to take place (centralized or decentralized) to best move the organization toward success. Organization structure is typically either vertical or horizontal in nature.

5   Explain the contextual dimensions of an organization.

Organizations exist to provide products and services in an extremely competitive environment. In order to survive and even surpass their competitors, an organization's leaders must determine that which they can do better than any other establishment: their competitive advantage. A competitive advantage is achieved when an organization selects and implements a strategy that effectively uses the resources and processes supported by the structure of the organization. Strategic competitiveness is what a firm achieves when it creates a value-centered environment where everyone contributes.

Once the organization's leaders have studied the environments in which they intend to compete, the next step they take is to create a vision and mission for the organization. A vision statement gives the organization an ultimate goal for which to strive. A vision intends to capture the values and aspirations of everyone associated with the company in hopes of engaging all of the stakeholder's in the long-term strategy. It is the ultimate responsibility of the CEO to work with others on his or her staff to form the vision for the organization.

6   Why are stakeholders critical to an organization's success?

Organizations, in general, have numerous ways to measure and improve their efficiency primarily by using information technology. It is safe to say that efficiency can be addressed in a quantitative fashion. Effectiveness can be difficult to assess; it is a qualitative issue because it often depends on the expectations of the organization's stakeholders. A stakeholder is any group, inside or outside of the organization, who has a vested interest in the organization's outcomes.

7   What is the relationship between team goals and organizational goals?

The work performed by teams and groups within an organization is composed of tasks that are of strategic importance to the organization. Project teams especially serve to improve horizontal communication throughout the organization. Trends in organizational design over the past decades have increasingly resulted in the development and implementation of teams.

The traditional or vertical structure of organizations, although great for providing controls, poses far too many challenges in efficiencies and effectiveness to the organization's success. The organizations that have embraced teamwork are able to profit from delegation of authority, quicker responses to the changing environment and empowerment of those employees in lower levels to make their own decisions.

Organizations, in general, use two types of teams in achieving strategic goals. One type of team is the cross-functional team. Members of cross-functional teams usually continue to report to their functional department while also reporting to the team to which they are assigned. This approach usually works best for implementing change throughout the organization or for new product development.

Permanent teams, the other type of team approach, also focus on information sharing and communication. The difference between permanent teams and cross-functional teams is that permanent teams stay together to focus on specific tasks. These teams consist of members who have the knowledge, skills, abilities and authority to manage their own work.

Cross-functional teams and permanent teams are two high level descriptions of how members of an organization work in the context of organizational design.

Appendix: Chapter 7 Answers to Review Questions

1   Discuss ethics principles and practices in business.

Ethics is, simply stated, about decisions and behavior with regard to right and wrong—as individuals, in groups and teams, within organizations and within society in general. Business ethics, also simply stated, is about the decisions we make and how we behave with regard to what is right and wrong as business individuals, in business groups and teams, within business organizations and within society in general.

Kirk Hanson, the executive director of the Markula Center for Applied Ethics at Santa Clara University, suggests five ways to think about ethics. He refers to these principles as "traditions with practical application" These are Hanson's five ways to think about ethics:

*   Is the proposed behavior promoting the greatest good?
*   Is the proposed behavior honoring the legitimate rights/human rights of individuals and groups?
*   Will all parties be treated fairly?
*   Is the behavior in line with accepted/traditional virtues?
*   Is the common good adequately served?

2   Why is it important to understand the relationship between ethics, the law and free choice?

A template does not truly exist when it comes to ethics. These are basic guidelines, and each situation should be handled on its own merits. Nevertheless, the five suggestions stated above give some structure to instill a sense of consistency for ethical decision making.

In the work environment, employees from many different backgrounds were raised with a variety of values and have a multitude of experiences upon which they draw to make daily decisions. These factors are only a few of the variables that make ethics difficult to define. Ethical dilemmas arise every day in personal, group and organization environments. An ethical dilemma is a situation in which right and wrong are difficult to identify, and all of the choices for resolution of the dilemma tend to have less than ultimate results.

A pending decision may create an ethical dilemma in one environment, and the same circumstance may be a common practice in another environment. A bribe, for example, can be illegal in one environment. Yet, in another environment, bribes might be a common practice. In this example, the choices and behaviors range from what is legal to what is free choice. Experts in the study of ethics describe this range of choices in a continuum, from legal to free choice, with ethical decision making midway between the two extremes.

According to Dr. Richard Daft, a management professor at Vanderbilt University, human behavior falls into the following three categories: legal, ethical and personal or free will. The standards by which the behaviors are measured range from the laws of the jurisdiction to the choices of individuals. The standard for ethics, which lies somewhere between legal statutes and free choice, is based on morals, values and principles. Individuals who fail to recognize and use morals and values as a tool for making ethical decisions tend to see every situation as, "if it's not illegal, it must be ethical".

3   Describe the principles of social responsibility. Why are these principles an important aspect of an organization's strategy?

Corporate Social Responsibility

Organizations establish their stance on differentiating right from wrong through corporate social responsibility (CSR) programs. CSR is the organization's commitment to make decisions that will benefit society as well as the organization.

The primary model of CSR contains four domains of responsibility: economic, legal, ethical and philanthropic. Together, the four criteria provide the social responsibility benchmarks for a company's level of response to CSR expectations.

Economic CSR

In the past, an organization's economic responsibility was limited to making a profit for the company and its stakeholders. A purely profit-oriented approach is no longer acceptable in the United States, Canada and Europe in efforts to deter corruption in business dealings.

Legal CSR

An organization's legal social responsibilities include adherence to local, state and federal laws. Some of the examples included in an organization's legal social responsibility include avoiding fraud, defective good, unnecessary services and inflated billing practices.

Ethical CSR

Ethical responsibilities of organizations include making ethical decisions. An organization is described as ethical when its profits and successes do not occur at the expense of other organizations or individuals.

Philanthropic CSR

Philanthropic responsibility, also known as discretionary responsibility, is quantified by the organization's voluntary contributions. This is the highest level of corporate social responsibility in that it goes beyond legal and social expectation. The main purpose of philanthropic responsibility is to contribute to society by giving back to the immediate community.

4   Define sustainability and why it is important.

Corporate responsibility can be summarized with one word: *sustainability*. Sustainability refers to how an organization strives for economic development and earnings in the current environment while taking into account the needs of future generations as well.

In 1994, John Elkington, a British consultant who founded his business and named it SustainAbility, coined the phrase "the triple bottom line." Since the early 1990s, business people like Mr. Elkington have argued that a company's true measure of success should be based on more than the traditional bottom line of profit and loss. The triple bottom line, according to Elkington, consists of three "Ps": profit, people and planet. In addition to measuring an organization's financial standing, two other aspects need measuring as well: social responsibility and environmental responsibility. The result of measuring the three Ps can then be truly equated to an organization's balanced scorecard.

Although the push for attention to the triple bottom line began with some enthusiasm and interest, it was followed by a decline in corporate social responsibility and economic chaos. There is now a resurgence of interest and support of corporate social responsibility. One example is the Global 100, which is an organization that began in 2005 with the purpose of identifying the top 100 most sustainable companies in the world. The criteria used by Global 100 include:

1 Energy productivity
2 Greenhouse gas productivity
3 Water productivity
4 Waste productivity
5 Innovation capacity
6 Percentage taxes paid
7 CEO to average employee pay
8 Safety productivity
9 Employee turnover
10 Leadership diversity
11 Clean capitalism paylink

Renewed interest and participation in corporate social responsibility begins with senior management and affects every employee of the organization. Many studies are beginning to identify the struggles and successes of companies that are including the three Ps in strategic management planning and other initiatives.

5 Apply ethics principles to establishing an ethical environment. Explain how to develop an ethical environment in the workplace.

Creating an Ethical Environment

Ethical dilemmas occur on a daily basis, in every environment and with varying results. Some ethical dilemmas go seemingly unnoticed while others deliver power consequences. In successful organizations, the strategic planning process includes goals and objectives designed to create and sustain an ethical environment. Individuals who are hired by organizations come from different parts of the world, with varying sets of values and backgrounds. Setting goals and objectives for an ethical environment provides a set of norms for all employees. A general "to do" list of critical items for an ethical environment begins with the following:

1　Establish an enforceable code of conduct
2　Initial and ongoing training
3　Regular communications
4　Anonymous reporting hotline
5　Enforcement/action
6　Reward employees that live the culture

Code of Conduct

Richard Thornburgh, a former U.S. Attorney General said, "Subordinates cannot be left to speculate as to the values of the organization. Top leadership must give forth clear and explicit signals, lest any confusion or uncertainty exist over what is and is not permissible conduct. To do otherwise allows informal and potentially subversive 'codes of conduct' to be transmitted with a wink and a nod, and encourages an inferior ethical system based on 'going along to get along' or the notion that 'everybody's doing it'."

A code of conduct serves as a guide and reference for all employees of an organization for making decisions about day to day activities. The code includes the company's mission, vision, values, principles and other standards of ethical and professional conduct. Responsible organizations use the code of conduct to encourage and enhance relationships between employees, the community and other stakeholders.

The Ethics Resource Center offers the following tips for writing a code of conduct for an organization:

1　Think in terms of values, beliefs and expectations rather than facts.
2　Keep it simple.
3　Be concise.
4　Use active voice rather than passive voice.
5　Give examples when it is appropriate.
6　Write so that others can understand—they are not experts in this area.
7　Do not attempt to write polished prose; keep updating your draft.
8　Read your work aloud to yourself.
9　Make your writing look easy to read.
10　Have others, especially your harshest critics, read what you have written.

Appendix: Chapter 8 Answers
to Review Questions

1   Define and describe the decision-making process.

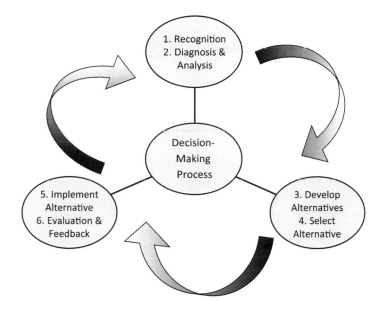

Figure 8.2

2   Review basic decision-making alternatives.

Decision-making practices will vary, depending on the work environment. In today's fast-paced economy, business and other professionals find themselves in situations that require quick actions, and these include making quick and wise decisions. While the decision-making process discussed earlier in this chapter is fundamental to learning effective decision-making skills, there comes a time when decision makers must rely more on quicker, yet reliable, methods.

The decision-making process and other traditional decision making models focus on problems and past events which caused problems. Current thinking about making decisions is beginning to focus more on possibilities and future desired outcomes. One model, created by Bostrom and associates, is called outcome-directed thinking. The research in this approach to decision making indicates that the use of outcome-directed thinking tends to illicit more creative ideas, more positive reactions and more optimism from those who use this approach.

3   How can you determine the best decision making alternative to use?

Decisions are faced and made every day. Some decisions are easier to make than others; yet, all decisions have consequences. The purpose of including decision making in Chapter 8 is to provide some guidelines for consistent and effective decision-making practices. This chapter will include group decision making practices in addition to general comments from current research on this invaluable skill.

A practical approach to decision making might suggest three possible alternatives: ignore the issue, quickly get rid of the issue or address the issue through sound decision-making practices. While ignoring and disposing of the issue quickly tend to make the issue more complex, taking a structured decision making approach can yield richer results.

4   Define and describe some decision-making pitfalls.

Answer: Decision Making Pitfalls

Although working in groups and teams has many benefits, it is important to raise awareness of the potential pitfalls. There are five key areas for groups and teams to watch in order to avoid negative impacts on their progress. The five key areas include groupthink, escalation of commitment, the Abilene Paradox, group polarization and unethical decision making.

Groupthink

Definition: Groupthink occurs when members of a group fail to express opinions that oppose those of other members of the group. Groupthink results from the desire of group members to maintain unity and harmony within the group members versus making the best decision possible.

Example: A group/team is assigned to develop a new process for the production of a new product. As the group approaches the end of the project, a member of another department shares information with a member of the group that could potentially affect the group's progress. The group member does not place importance on the new information because of loyalty to the group, assuming that the group has to be right in their findings.

Symptoms: Some of the most common symptoms of groupthink include:

- Feeling invulnerable
- Believing the group has ultimate morality
- Feeling pressure to dissent
- Rationalizing with the group by being biased

Potential consequences of groupthink include:

- Failure to review all alternative solutions
- Biased choices
- Limited search of information
- Lack of alternative plans

Tips for teams: Avoid groupthink by following these suggestions:

- Limit group size; form subgroups if necessary
- Share concerns privately writing down comments anonymously
- Invite team members to role play opposing positions
- Appoint someone to be a devil's advocate

Escalation of Commitment

Definition: Escalation of commitment occurs when a team continues to invest resources on an effort in spite of feedback that the solution is not effective.

Example: The group receives feedback about the solution to a problem. The feedback indicates that the solution is not working. Instead of "pulling the plug" on the project, the group continues in efforts to fix the solution, while the negative feedback continues.

Symptoms: The primary symptoms of escalation of commitment include:

- Negative feedback
- Increased cost
- Additional needed resources

Potential consequences of escalation of commitment include:

- Wasted resources
- Lack of approval
- Failure
- Dismissal from employment

Tips for teams:

- Set limits early on
- Avoid tunnel vision
- Be realistic about costs and resources
- Invite outsider's feedback

The Abilene Paradox

Definition: Groupthink and escalation of commitment tend to be the result of individual behavior in groups/teams. The Abilene Paradox is about team behavior that occurs when all of the members attempt to avoid conflict and end up with a result that no one wanted. With the Abilene Paradox, team members make decisions they believe other members want.

Example: The Abilene Paradox is named after an actual event that occurred in Texas. A group of individuals take a trip to Abilene, in extreme heat, with no air-conditioning to a restaurant for dinner. Once there, each individual expresses their dissatisfaction with the entire trip, the meal and other circumstances. They find out that no one wanted to make the trip; yet, each individual agreed to go because they believed the other members of the group wanted to go.

Symptoms:

- A member of the group is perceived to be an expert of some type.
- Lack of confidence
- Pressure to conform
- Dysfunctional behavior within the group

Potential consequences of the Abilene Paradox include:

- Failure to achieve team goals
- Loss of time and other resources
- Resentment
- Dissention from group norms

Tips for teams:

- Confront issues in a team setting
- Vote privately on issues

- Establish a forum for controversial issues
- Failure is a possibility; take responsibility

Unethical Decision Making

Definition: Unethical decision making occurs when the pressure of group-think, escalation of commitment and other biases creates an environment in which groups make decisions contrary to the benefit of the group and the organization. Unethical decision making is typically the result of a series of events as opposed to a single event.

Example: After receiving negative feedback on a group's project or solution, the group tries to cover up or misuse information to deflect blame or gain an undeserved advantage.

Symptoms:

- Lack of accountability
- Lies and withholding of information
- Secret meetings and alliances
- Lack of progress

Potential consequences of unethical decision making include:

- Illegal activity
- Failure
- Dissention
- Whistle-blowing

Tips for teams:

- Avoid and/or eliminate conflicts of interest
- Tell the truth
- Create an environment of integrity
- Communicate

Appendix: Chapter 9 Answers to Review Questions

1   Review time-management principles by comparing Cheryl Clausen's and Kathy Peel's perspectives.

Sales coach Cheryl Clausen states her interpretation of time management by first stating that she hates the term *time management*. Clausen's believes it is not about managing time but rather about managing the way we use our time. While some time management experts believe that time management is about tracking time by writing everything down in a calendar or planner, Clausen believes managing our time is about the following steps:

- Setting clear objectives.
- Identifying what needs to occur to produce the objectives.
- Tracking successful actions and results.
- Being at the right place at the right time.
- Sticking to the plan while being prepared for the unexpected.

Kathy Peel is a family manager and coach who shares her thoughts about time management in her blog. Her list of time management realities include the following suggestions[4]:

- No perfect planning system exists.
- While no system is perfect, no system at all is crazy.
- Plan; you can't predict.
- Know your personal priorities.
- Life is more about rhythm than balance.
- Know your own rhythm for your life.

2   What did you learn about Dr. Wetmore's time-management myth?

Perhaps Dr. Donald E. Wetmore of the Productivity Institute says it best. He has conducted over 2,000 seminars and workshops on the time-management myth during the past 30 years. He believes most of our stress is due to unrealistic expectations we set for ourselves in thinking we can do everything that needs to be done. Dr. Wetmore says, "It is instructive that when we go to the funeral home to pay our respects to a dear departed friend, the focus is always on what that person did in their lives, not what they did not do. We celebrate one another's achievements and do not bemoan what they did not do. Yet, in our own lives many task themselves over what they are not doing, what they have not accomplished." Clearly, our focus needs to shift to what we can do instead of what we did not do by directing our energy toward those accomplishments that are most valuable to each of us.

3   Analyze time-management issues in daily activities by describing whether you agree or disagree with the six most important things you need to know about time management.
   1   Time is a nonrenewable resource.
   2   Time is either used effectively or wasted.
   3   Multitasking is a myth.
   4   Wasting time causes stress.
   5   Practice saying no.
       •   Fear of offending
       •   Caught off guard
       •   Feel needed
       •   Lack of goals and objectives (others will determine for you)
       •   Fear of letting down your boss or other team members
   6   Balancing time between work and personal life is important to your health.

4   Describe the six most common time wasters, and discuss your view on how useful this list is in learning time-management techniques.
   1   Anything that does not contribute directly to your goals and objectives.
   2   Lack of concentration.
   3   Too many meetings.
   4   Interruptions
       •   Set a time limit
       •   Encourage stand-up meetings

- Set appointments
- Avoid unnecessary conversation
- Avoid those who continually take advantage
- If asked, "Got a minute?". . . say no

5 Multitasking
6 Procrastination
- Lack of self-discipline
- Convincing yourself that you work better under pressure
- Lack of deadlines
- Failure to monitor your progress
- Doings easy tasks first; postponing the difficult tasks
- Unrealistic time estimates
- Trying to do too much

5 Do you share monochronic or polychronic time management values? Why is this important while working with people from different cultures?

The value of knowing the characteristics listed is twofold. It is as important to understand your personal time management values as it is to understand time management values of those form other cultures with whom you might work in a group or team.

6 Briefly describe the relationship between time management and stress.

Stress impacts a life well lived on so many levels. The American Institute of Stress reports that stress is America's number one health problem". In January, 2012, the American Psychological Association (APA) published its yearly survey results on stress in America, indicating a "deepening concern about

Table 9.1

Monochronic Values	Polychronic Values
Tend to do one thing at a time	Do several things at the same time
Are not easily distracted	Are susceptible to distractions
Commit to work	Commit to relationships
Place importance on deadlines	Place less importance on deadlines
Stick to plans	Change plans often and easily
Value and respect privacy	Value connection
Relate punctuality to reputation	Relate punctuality to the relationship
Accept short-term relationships	Lean toward lifetime relationships

the connections between chronic disease and stress." The most current survey does indicate that Americans are beginning to recognize the link between stress and illness; yet, little is being done to correct the situation. The APA suggests that a lack of effective time management might be the most significant reason underlying the lack of positive change.

7   Discuss the pros and cons of a dependence on technology for time management.

Plenty of research exists on the effectiveness of technology when it comes to time management. The software industry has provided numerous tools for the consumer, and the trend continues to expand. Recently, a *Business Week* article suggested that the "very digital tools we count on to be more productive can also drag down our efficiency when they're used too much." *The Business Week* special report also includes information about the cost of time-management issues. Specifically, digital interruptions in the work environment reportedly take up to 25% of the average worker's day and cost $650 billion a year in lost productivity. Up to 44% of technology users time is spent on instant messaging, e-mail and social networking.

Appendix: Chapter 10 Answer to Review Question

Develop a personal lifelong learning plan.

1 Where are you now with regard to your future needs?
2 Where do you need to be in the future?
3 How do you get there?

Twenty Steps to Cultivate Lifelong Learning

1 **Books:** Always have a book to read a little at a time.
2 **Lists:** Keep a "to learn" list of things you have always wanted to learn.
3 **Think:** Get more intellectual friends; people who like to think and learn.
4 **Guided thinking:** Spend time journaling, meditating or reflecting on ideas.
5 **Practice:** Apply your knowledge by doing something with the information you have learned.
6 **Teach:** Communicate your ideas to others by teaching, starting a blog, mentoring someone or simply discussing ideas with a friend.
7 **Focus on what counts:** There is so much information available today that it is important to focus on what counts.
8 **Learn in groups:** Join organizations, take workshops and make learning a social experience.
9 **Unlearn assumptions:** Challenge your way of thinking by seeking out information that opposes your views.
10 **Find jobs that encourage learning:** Consider a job and career that encourages intellectual freedom.

11   **Start a project:** Set out to do something new, and learn from the experience.

12   **Follow your intuition:** Stretch your imagination by listening to your "gut feeling."

13   **The morning 15:** Use the first 15 minutes of the day to learn something.

14   **Reap the rewards:** Learn information that is useful in your daily activities.

15   **Make it a priority:** Give lifelong learning the importance you want it to have.

16   **Have fun:** Productivity and having fun are not mutually exclusive concepts.

17   **Find your rhythm:** Make it a point to spend time working as well as relaxing. Instead of trying to find a balance between working and relaxing, try finding your rhythm.

18   **Travel:** Discover new places and enrich your life with different perspectives.

19   **Socialize:** Spend time with others on a social level for no other reason than to catch up on each other's lives.

20   **Give back:** Volunteer, share and give back to others.

Index